Harry

Truman

The Man Who Divided the World

(Harry Truman and the Four Months That Changed the World)

Jack Brunt

Published By **Ryan Princeton**

Jack Brunt

All Rights Reserved

Harry Truman: The Man Who Divided the World (Harry Truman and the Four Months That Changed the World)

ISBN   978-1-990373-90-9

Legal & Disclaimer

Table Of Contents

Chapter 1: Early Presidents Facts

George Washington (1789-1797)

Washington was the sole single, unanimously elected US president. He refused to accept the salary of the President, even though at the time, the $25,000 salary was a huge amount of money.

George Washington did not live in the White House. The capital was situated in Philadelphia along with other cities during the time Washington was the president. Washington was the only president that was not a member of a political group.

Washington was unable to attend his inaugural ceremony as President in which case he took a loan of 600 dollars from his neighbor to make it.

It has been a debate for a long time between historians about whether

Washington might not have be the first President to put the words "so help me god" at the conclusion of the oath the President swears. It is instead said that the first president to alter the phrase to include the phrase was Chester Alan Arthur. The phrase was changed after having been sworn into office after Garfield's passing in 1881.

Washington wasn't George Washington's first name. De Wessyngton was his first name Washington used as his surname. It was given to him by his uncle who was a Knight of the Order from the 12th century. The uncle was named William de Hertburn. He was the manor's keeper located in Wessyngton. Then, later in his life He chose to add a new spelling in his surname. Eventually, it changed into de Wessyngton that's how Normans used to pronounce Washington.

The Washington's teeth were constructed of wood. However, in reality they were composed out of tusks from a walrus, and an elephant. Also, they had brackets made of gold.

Washington created a drink to all his guests on Mount Vernon that consisted of the whiskey rye, peach brandy and, of course, an apple brandy. The drink was made in the private distillery of Washington.

Washington was elected by a majority vote. That means that all voters were able to vote for Washington.

John Adams (1797-1801)

Adams enjoyed taking a take a skinny plunge into the Potomac River quite often. It helped him deal with the stress of being President. He would go for an early morning dip around 5 a.m.

Adams decided to go hunting or fish in lieu of school as a child.

Adams when he ran against Jefferson declared that, if Jefferson won the election, Adams would instruct "robbery, incest, murder, adultery, and rape to the constituents." They became close friends later and sent many letters to one another throughout the course of their lives.

The first President to reside in the White House.

The day he died was the same in the same year as Jefferson and also happens to coincide with the 50th anniversary of the Declaration.

Thomas Jefferson (1801-1809)

Thomas Jefferson as well as John Adams traveled to see Shakespeare's birthplace in Stratford-upon-Avon. They took an axe from their pockets, and cut off

Shakespeare's chair, to be able to bring clips back as a memento.

Jefferson was one of the founding fathers of Virginia University in 1819. He established it in the property of the President of the time, Monroe.

Thomas Jefferson was the first president to serve in Washington, DC.

Jefferson enjoyed a long-running relationship with his wife's half-sister, Sally Hemings. She also served as the child of the family. Their relationship was a long time as well as the proof of his being the father of her children is frequently questioned. In 1998, DNA tests revealed that a member of the family of Jefferson was actually the father of one child she was born with. This only showed that the bloodline of his father was responsible for the child and not necessarily directly.

Jefferson wasn't well-known as a writer until his demise when his daughter found and published the novel which he composed about the virtues of Jesus and the lack of other qualities besides of being a brilliant thinker.

Jefferson was a believer in the old wives' tails, and would bathe his feet in cold water with belief that he'd never get an illness.

Jefferson's last words to his friend included "this is the 4th?"

Jefferson created his own epitaph and in it, he referred to his contribution to the Declaration and the Statuette for the Protection of Religious freedom in Virginia. In addition, he mentioned that he was the founder president of Virginia University. He totally forgot about the presidency.

Jefferson was fluent in six different languages.

Jefferson was the inventor of the first chair that swiveled.

The public speaker was so dreadful often that, during his time as President the President only made two speeches. It was one speech each period he was in office.

He initiated with the State of the Union process in which the documents are sent to Congress for reading by a secretary.

Jefferson was studying to become meteorologist. He would write down the temperature of his journals every day for two days. He also kept track of the pattern of rain.

Jefferson wasn't just president, but was also a skilled architect. He designed and constructed his home at Monticello. Additionally, he built buildings to support Virginia University.

James Madison (1809-1817)

Madison as well as Jefferson were in the same room while they were detained after taking a carriage ride across the rolling countryside of Vermont. It was an unofficial Sunday and, in the time of Jefferson and Madison it was prohibited.

Madison finished her undergraduate studies in just two years, and then stayed one year longer to pursue her studies.

Madison who was 5'4" is actually the most diminutive President ever to have been elected. In addition, he did not weigh more than 100 pounds.

Madison was Princeton's first graduate at Princeton.

Madison faced financial difficulties following his departure from the presidency.

Madison was a wheat farmer and also an agriculturalist within the city of

Montpelier, Virginia. Weather conditions and the insects affected his crops, and reduced costs for his market share.

The stepson of Madison also depleted his savings, putting the family in financial trouble.

James Monroe (1817-1825)

Monroe was once so angry over the Secretary of State that he chased him across in the White House with fire tongs.

Monroe was acknowledged by the capital of Liberia which is named his honor, and its moniker being Monrovia.

Monroe was a fan of extravagant clothes, which were old-fashioned Revolutionary War era style clothing. The nickname he earned for himself was "the last cocked hat."

Monroe's first term evoked such a feelings of nationalism that it was dubbed the Era of Good Feelings. It was the result of the war of 1812.

Monroe was unopposed in his second term, which occurred only once more when he was with George Washington.

The death occurred 55 years following when the Declaration of Independence was signed and incorporated into the Congress.

Monroe was a supporter of Monroe's support for the American Colonization Society that freed slaves from Liberia.

Even though Monroe was elected as the 5th President, he became the 3rd President who died on July 4th.

Monroe loved to travel, on mules when he went from Paris as well as Madrid.

Monroe went to Spain in order to aid in gaining the right to inherit Florida free from the Spanish sway in 1805. The mule, however, and his visit to Spain was not enough to win Spain's heart.

John Quincy Adams (1825-1829)

Adam's last words as he passed away included "Thomas Jefferson still lives" in part because he was not conscious of the fact that Jefferson died just a couple of hours earlier.

John Quincy Adams was the son of John Adams.

Adams was in favor of an expedition towards the middle of the Earth. But, Jackson vetoed the approval after he took office four years following the approval was signed.

An interviewer once was seated in the middle of Adams clothing and would not allow him to leave until he was able to conduct an interview with Adams.

Andrew Jackson (1829-1837)

Jackson was the first president that was rewarded with an attempted assassination aimed toward Jackson. It is Richard Lawrence, who painted houses. Both guns malfunctioned which had an odds of 125,000 that this could occur. Jackson realizing that the person had no weapons was able to chase him off by walking his stick.

Jackson was president of the very first. He was actually the first person to travel on an automobile.

Andrew Jackson hated the use of currency made from paper. He believed in gold and silver far more. In fact, he stopped down the Second Bank of the US in part due to his apprehension about the manipulative nature of paper money.

Jackson was a fan of a parrot who was cursed by those near. When Jackson was buried the bird needed be taken away due to the profanity.

Jackson has killed one man during a fight.

Jackson was born into the state that is now one of the Carolinas. Jackson was extremely intelligent, but extremely unsure.

Jackson was wounded in the chest. He stayed on the ground to shoot, and then killed his adversaries. The bullet remained within his chest for over 40 years.

Martin Van Buren (1837-1841)

The word "OK" is due to the presidency of Martin Van Buren who carried the moniker"Old Kinderhook" "Old Kinderhook". The reason for this was his being born and raised within Kinderhook, New York. The political parties began to come out with the name "OK" in an effort to help van Buren campaign.

Martin Van Buren was a United States citizen of natural birthright. This made Martin Van Buren the very first President to become a citizen. Every president before Van Buren were British peasants.

Van Buren penned his own autobiography, and Van Buren did not even refer to his long-time wife. He did not mention her a single time.

Jackson was involved in numerous fights against other men in the name of the wife Rachel. He was actually hit with multiple shots to his body and chest. The first was in 1806 while an additional one was 1813, and the final one was in 1813, when he was a Senator from Missouri Thomas Hart Benton.

Van Buren had many nicknames:

* Sly fox

* Red fox of Kinderhook

* Old Kinderhook

* Little Magician

He was fluent in English as his second or third language. The first language he spoke was Dutch.

William Henry Harrison (1841)

Harrison was the most lengthy inauguration speech ever in Presidential speeches. The speech contained 8 578 words. It took one hour and 40 minutes his speech to be complete. Even though he made his speech at the time of his inauguration however, the weather was extremely stormy the next month, and the cause of his death was due to pneumonia.

Harrison was the only person to serve a shorter period in office due to the death of.

Harrison owned an unusual pet He had an unusual pet, the Billy goat.

His presidency lasted for a total of 31 days.

Harrison was a target for haters who deemed his more likely to sit in a cabin or log and sip hard cider. To counter these Harrison made lemonade spiked and gave whiskey from Log cabin jugs to people who stood behind Harrison.

He was enrolled as an medical doctor prior to becoming a president.

Harrison was president from 9 to 23 and his grandson was the 23rd.

John Tyler (1841-1845)

The only President with more children than he could count on his fingers Tyler. He had eight children with his 1st wife, then seven more children with his second wife. The last of his children was born an old man of 70. The name of the baby was Pearl. Also, he was the first president to have a wedding within the White House while in office. The first eight children of his were not present or apropos of the wedding ceremony.

Tyler did not take over the Presidency following Harrison's death since no one was sure of the job he was going to play in his role as the Vice-President, that led to the system which we are still using in the present. The 25th Amendment was passed in the year 1898, allowing vice presidents to be appointed in the event that the President had no longer the capacity to.

John Tyler was an amazing violinist. He performed at parties for entertaining guests. He wanted to be a performer at concerts.

Everyone was against Tyler. Tyler even was exiled from a party that was supportive of the president during his time as President. His cabinet, which was comprised of just one member decided to quit because of the rules were implemented by him. The president was impeached, which made him the first facing it.

Even newspapers rebuked the man by calling the president an "miserable and imbecile" who has been sluggish and petty. The New York Times called the president "the most unpopular President which has ever held that office within the US." The post was inserted into the obituary, when it was released.

Lincoln did not make any funeral proclamations, or even drop the flag at the time Tyler was killed because of the hatred everyone felt towards him.

Two grandsons from Tyler live on today. A son was born in 1924 while the other one was born in 1928.

James K. Polk (1845-1849)

The first president serving the country from coast west to coast.

Polk prohibited dancing, alcohol and playing cards out of his White House.

Polk was considered to be an underdog.

Polk promised that he would not run again in the event of his being elected to the first time.

The name he got is Young Hickory.

The first President American president. Dark Horse Presidents.

Because Van Buren failed to gain the nomination, Polk ended up being nominated and later was elected.

Polk was the first president to get an image of him taken.

Zachary Taylor (1849-1850)

Zachary Taylor told the Mexican general Santa Ana to go to hell after he demanded his fellow Americans surrender.

Taylor was selected as the Wig candidate for the Wig Taylor was not notified. The Wig Party tried to contact him by the letter, but they did not cover the cost of postage. Consequently, after he rejected the notice, he was not know about his election.

Taylor's nickname was old-fashioned rough, sloppy, and prepared. Taylor got his nickname from his behavior during his time fighting the Seminoles.

He didn't actually vote to the Presidential elections before his or even after his.

Zachary Taylor had a ravenous appetite. When he was celebrating the 4th of July the man ate a sack of cherries and then drank an iced drink to wash the food down. The event took place near in the area where Washington Monument is now. Washington Monument now stands.

Because of the cherry juice and milk that contained bacteria, he passed away just a few days after.

Zachary Taylor was considered to be tough.

Taylor together with fifty other sick men battled against a tribe of six Native Americans.

Millard Fillmore (1850-1853)

Under Fillmore's presidency, the president made use of a stove and water to run the White House. This was the first time to The White House and the Presidents.

Fillmore was a lover of reading and reading. He created a library at the White House that has become permanently. He also battled the fire which threatened to ruin the library after it was threatened with destruction. White House burned down then approved a bill to repair all books taken away from the White House.

Fillmore was far more enthusiastic about the school system than many people ever since the day he got married to his teacher at school.

The official website of the White House calls Fillmore an insufferable man.

The first president to have a step-mother.

Fillmore was the only one of four presidents who didn't have a Vice President during the time of his presidency. The law that allowed for the Vice President to be replaced in the event of the death of a President or his departure, was implemented in the year 1967. It was during this time in which the ratification of 25th amendment was made.

Franklin Pierce (1853-1857)

He was a brilliant memory-keeper. He remembered his speech from the inaugural completely, including the entire 3,319 words.

Pierce didn't swear in to the office by placing his hands on a law book, but instead he used the bible.

Peirce was an extremely unpopular president. Peirce was so insecure that his party quit the presidency and was unable to nominate his successor at the conclusion of his presidency. In response, he said, "I've nothing left to do but get drunk."

He was a sly drinker and drove over an older woman on his horse.

James Buchanan (1857-1861)

James Buchanan was known to buy slaves in Washington D.C., without anyone being aware. Then, he would allegedly take his slaves to Pennsylvania in order to release them. But, many dispute the claim, claiming that he did actually take the animals home to use as a way to look after the home he was living in.

He was a single man. He was President and was the only president who wasn't married. But, he was close to William R. King who was a senator from Alabama. Alabama Senator. They would appear everywhere, and they were nicknamed the most gender-specific names, i.e. Mr. and Mrs.

Buchanan employed his niece to serve as White House hostess.

Buchanan resided with Senator Buchanan's closest friend for over 10 years. It raised doubts about his sexuality.

King, his friend King, his companion France in 1844, with his companion King. Buchanan was reported to have said "I am now alone and solitary." He further claimed that he'd attempted to charm a number of men however none would have accepted his advances.

Abraham Lincoln (1861-1865)

The toys Lincoln Logs have the name that comes from Abraham Lincoln and the hut that he was born in. John Lloyd Wright, son of famous designer Francis Lloyd Wright, invented the Lincoln Logs.

Lincoln was able to launch an attack preemptively by establishing the secret services only to end up dying a short time after. At the moment, they were conducting an investigation into fake currency.

Lincoln was the sole President who ran for his election in 1859 who wasn't a freemason.

The King of Siam attempted to offer the gift of elephants to Lincoln but he refused with respect.

The very first president to be given photos at the time of his inauguration was Abraham Lincoln. In the photograph, Lincoln was right alongside his assassin John Wilkes Booth.

Lincoln was the President to come from outside the 13 original colonies.

Lincoln was the first president to be granted the US patent for the invention he invented. The patent's number is #6469.

Lincoln became the first president who wore beards. The beard was a result of the suggestion of a young little girl called Gracie Bedell.

Lincoln's son Willie aged 12, at the time of his death was the first of Lincoln's children to pass away while at the White House.

Lincoln was the president with the highest height. Lincoln was 6'4 tall".

Abraham Lincoln's mom died because the family's cow was taking in some plants which were poisonous. Then afterward, she consumed the milk of the cow. It was a white snakeroot plant.

The first president to be assassinated.

Lincoln was a wrestler who had a passion for it. He took home several wins, up to 300, or more to be exact.

He proclaimed his Emancipation Proclamation and abolished the slave trade.

Lincoln received his Wrestling Hall of Fames Outstanding American award.

Lincoln used to be a construction worker who was cutting rails down for fencing.

Lincoln was afraid about being assassinated He told his bodyguards on the day he was killed.

Abraham Lincoln, as a licensed bartender would serve alcohol-based drinks to his guests and relatives, and also serve as president. He was a owners of Berry and Lincoln, a establishment that opened within Springfield, Illinois.

Lincoln kept things inside his stove-pipe cap. The items included documents, letters as well as other items of importance.

Andrew Johnson (1865-1869)

Andrew Johnson, who was also a tailor, was the sole professional tailor who was President. In his presidency, he stopped making tailoring orders to carry out his duties as President. He only wore clothes and suits he designed by himself.

Johnson was drinking during his own inaugural.

Johnson was impeached, which made Johnson the first person to go through this. Johnson was acquitted with a single, one-person decision that was endorsed by the Senate chairperson. After that, it took 130 years before he was again subject to impeachment. This was in the year Bill Clinton received his impeachment.

Johnson upon his requests, was interred by his request, was buried with the America Flag wrapped around him as well as a copy of the Constitution.

Johnson and his brother, were sent out to become the son of a servant after his father died. The two brothers worked as servants for an tailor. They gained enough experience to design their own clothes. Two years later the two boys fled and went on to be individual lives. The tailor only offered $10 as a reward for their return to the two boys. However, no one accepted this promise.

Ulysses S. Grant (1869-1877)

Grant was such a prolific smokeer that he was believed to consume 20 cigarettes per every day. After the US were victorious in war, the country provided him with 10,000 cigars which was later used to smoke. In later years, Grant was diagnosed with throat cancer, and passed away.

Grant gave an Presidential pardon Samuel Mudd, who was the doctor who was responsible for taking care of Booth's injured ankle. Booth later killed Lincoln in the Ford Theater.

Grant's inauguration Grant was to be a time when canaries perform, however due to the cold weather the birds froze and died.

He was sentenced to a fine of $30 for speeding the carriage and horse.

Grant was the guest of honor for the theater where Lincoln was killed in. He was convinced that he could've prevented the incident and was guilt-ridden for the rest of his life.

Grant felt dizzy at his sight of blood that's odd considering Grant was a soldier in Civil War. Civil War.

Grant ended his involvement in the Ku Klux Klan during his presidency, however they returned over the course of many years.

Rutherford B. Hayes (1877-1881)

In his early years, Hayes fought off lyssophobia as it is a anxiety of becoming insane.

Hayes was an anti-prohibitionist, who prohibited drinking alcohol at the White

House during his Presidency. Hayes also hosted sing-alongs to gospel each evening.

Hayes used the very first phone at the White House. It is believed that he was one of the first people to make use of the phone, and his number was one.

Hayes did not win the popular vote by the difference in the range of 250,000. But the electoral college gave him the presidency by one vote. The result earned him the nickname for the Ruther fraud.

Hayes was instrumental in launching the very first Easter Egg Roll Hunt at the White House.

He was referred to as Granny Hayes because he did not support drinking tobacco, gambling, or smoking.

Hayes was shot four times in his time in the Civil War and subsequently lost four horses due because of gunshot wounds, due to their being in his way.

Hayes contributed to the transfer of a significant part of Paraguay back to Paraguay after it was lost the country to Argentina as well as Brazil.

James A. Garfield (1881)

James A. Garfield spoke with Alexander Graham Bell over the phone. Garfield was the first president that could speak on the phone. Conversations took place across a distance of 13 miles and he would often declare, "Speak a little slower."

Garfield was killed at the back by Anarchist Charles Guiteau, who was also an attorney. He employed a five-barrel, .44-caliber pistol to assassinate Garfield. The gun was dubbed"the" British Bulldog. He confessed that he made a decision that he wanted to shoot this gun due to the fact that he believed this model was beautiful to display at an art gallery. The gun, however, was never recovered.

Even though Garfield didn't die of the wound from a gunshot in his back However, he passed away of complications resulting from the removal of the wound. Garfield's hands weren't well-maintained, and he developed an infection within the wound. He was in extreme amounts of pain for more than eight days, before dying. Then, Guiteau used this to gain advantage by claiming doctors were responsible for killing Garfield but not him.

He was gifted with the ability to write in different languages at the same time using both hands.

Garfield was a writer the poem in Greek as well as Latin.

The President was the first left-handed president elected president.

He was shot in the course of the Presidency, and it took him 11 weeks to bring his death. Doctors tried using the new metal detector, which was unable to detect the springs that were in the mattress. The result was numerous attempts to get the bullets in incorrect places, causing infection.

Chester Arthur (1881-1885)

He had 80 pairs of trousers that allowed him to change his clothing a few times in a single day.

Arthur desired a brand new coat of paint for the interior of the White House, so he offered 24 wagons filled with historic relics. It included Lincoln's pair pants as well as Adam's capes. The hats were not the only thing that Arthur was looking for. He was fond of elaborate clothes and owned more than 80 pairs of pants. The result was the name for his nickname of

Elegant Arthur. Also, he had an individual valet.

Arthur saw four women give their marriage vows on the day he ended his presidency.

Arthur was popularly known for his night-owlish behavior. Arthur would go for walks late at night, to take in DC landmarks often along with his friends. He would sometimes come back around three or four early in the morning.

Grover Cleveland (1885-1889, 1893-1897)

Grover Cleveland is the first president in history to have held the office of execution. This was before sheriff Erie County, New York and repeatedly a place of hanging.

The president Grover Cleveland is the first and only president to serve two terms which were not the same period. His first term was as president 14th and his second as the 22nd president.

Cleveland was married in The White House, making him the first person to be married during his presidency.

Cleveland was appointed the guardian legal of a 11-year-old girl who was his co-lawpartner's daughter. He died, and the law partner took custody of the girl. Ten years later then, he was able to wed her at the White House. She was the first youngest lady. She was just 21 when she became the first lady.

A portion of the jaw of Cleveland's face was constructed of rubber that was formed by vulcanization. It is because of his surgery on his yacht, which was kept secret.

Cleveland served as town sheriff of Erie County, NY.

Cleveland was assigned to open the trapdoor at two hangs of criminals during the sheriff's profession. He was dubbed the nickname as the Buffalo Hangman.

Grover Cleveland was diagnosed with a cancerous tumour removed from his mouth The epithelium has been placed displayed in the Mutter Museum in Philadelphia.

Benjamin Harrison (1889-1893)

He was the father of Harrison was exhumed but then stolen by robbers from the grave. The body of Harrison was then donated at the Medical College of Ohio located in Cincinnati. Later, it was found out that it had been used as a cadaver in training purposes, but was later used for burial when it was recovered.

The first time that a Christmas tree was hung within the White House with Christmas lights occurred during Harrison's

Presidency. Harrison was also the first president to install electricity within the White House.

He was the grandchild to William H. Harrison.

The Human Iceberg is the nickname that Harrison received. It was because of his rigidity with people.

He resisted touching the switches and outlets in worry of electric shock. He slept while keeping all the lights of the room turned on.

Chapter 2: Early 1900's President Facts

William McKinley (1897-1901)

McKinley was in an ambulance driven by an engine that was not required to be turned. It happened shortly after the shooting. He was taken to the hospital in an ambulance.

McKinley was killed by an anarchist. While getting away McKinley told the secret service not to permit anyone to harm the attacker. McKinley was of the opinion that the gunman be ignorant and naive.

McKinley made use of the phone during his campaign to connect with the people he was campaigning with.

The first president who used buttons as the campaign souvenirs he received.

McKinley was known to enjoy wearing carnations as they were believed to bring luck-in-the-air.

He was the first to give his body to a girl in a small town, the girl was killed a brief period of time after. The following week, he passed away.

Theodore Roosevelt (1901-1909)

The whole Family that belonged to Teddy Roosevelt, including his wife, had a pair of stilts.

Following the time that McKinley was shot dead, Roosevelt became the President at the age of 42. He was the youngest president because of being in default.

Roosevelt had a condition of Asthma. As the time was when there were no inhalers and particular treatment options, he had trouble as a child. If he worked out and tried to fight asthma, and ultimately overcome breathing difficulties.

The development of Teddy Bear was due to the actions of Roosevelt who refused to take a newborn bear that was on the open wild. The media picked up on this story, and the news prompted millions of people as in toy manufacturers to raise awareness by distributing stuffed animals.

Roosevelt gave the speech during his second presidential race when he was shot in the chest. Even though he was shot however, he carried on giving the speech completely. In the aftermath of the incident, he declared, "I do not know if you are aware that I have been shot, but I do not give a rap about that, not one rap." He then continued with the speech that lasted one hour and 30 minutes.

Roosevelt before his death went to heaven by saying his final words, which included "put out that light."

The mother of Roosevelt and his wife Roosevelt both died on Valentine's Day in 1884. The journalist wrote that it was the most horrible day he had ever experienced.

While he resided at the home of the president the house was not referred to as White House. Its name in the time was called the Presidential Palace Executive Mansion, and the President's House. Roosevelt named it the White House in 1901.

Roosevelt was the first to experience a vehicle ride in his presidency.

Roosevelt in irony was among the smallest to be elected President. He was 42 years old, 10, and only 18 days old.

Theodore suffered blindness in the left eye following an injury sustained during the boxing match.

William Howard Taft (1909-1913)

Taft was a hefty 325 pounds. and was known as Big Bill. Big Bill was the biggest-known President of all time. The President was often locked in baths at his White House. It was usually the responsibility of his advisors to lift his body out of the tub because he was stuck.

Taft took his bathtub on his trip from the United States to Panama. The reason for this was his adoration for baths.

Then, following his Presidency He swore in a number of other Presidency candidates.

* Coolidge

* Hoover

The country was served by him in two different ways.

1. President.

2. Supreme Court Chief Justice.

Hoover was the very first President born in an Western State. Hoover was raised in

Iowa and never been across Mississippi until in his early 20's.

Taft arrived at Presidency just following Teddy and other toy producers were worried about Teddy Bears becoming less appealing and so they created the toy upon Taft. This was Billy the Possum. This toy didn't get much attention.

Taft was a huge man in his presidency, but he lost about 80 pounds soon following the conclusion of his term. He lost 150 lbs. over the course of his presidency.

Woodrow Wilson (1913-1921)

Wilson was a golfer so passionately that his golf clubs would be sprayed black to match wintertime games. These balls could then be used to be observed during the winter.

Wilson presented the first film in The White House. It is The Birthing of a Nation. The film was banned afterward in time.

Wilson was awarded the Ph.D. The result was that he was the best educated president in the US. His education was Political Science as well as History at Johns Hopkins University. University of Johns Hopkins. The student was also able to take the bar exam in Georgia although the law school he attended was not completed.

Wilson was extremely theatrical. He always dreamed of appearing on the stage.

Wilson was afflicted with a series of strokes caused by stress during 1919. The result was that he became blind and partially paralyzed. He remained in office until 1921.

The wife of Wilson, Edith Bolling Galt, was a direct descendant from Pocahontas.

Wilson's iconic portrait is situated on the $100000 dollar currency that is seldom ever seen. These currencies were designed to facilitate commerce with Federal Reserve Banks. They went out of fashion after the development of the wire transfer method. There is a good chance that you would ever come across any of them again.

Wilson was a fervent sort of politician who advocated for democracy and the world's peace.

Wilson was the first President to be buried at Washington National Cathedral. Washington National Cathedral in Washington, DC.

Wilson was highly educated and highly educated professor in the academia.

Warren G. Harding (1921-1923)

In the wake of his obsession with gambling, he attempted to win and bet but lost his White House china for another man.

Harding made many history-making decisions in his presidency.

* The first radio station in the White House.

* The first speech that will be transmitted via radio broadcast.

* First president who rode in a vehicle to attend his own Induction.

* The first president elected in the aftermath of the passage of voting rights for women.

Harding was an avid philander. He was involved in relationships with a acquaintance of his wife as well as Nan Britton. Nan was later the author of the book that described what her daughter had done to be a descendants of Harding. In 2005, the man was confirmed as the father of kid by testing DNA.

Harding got married to a divorcee who was a father of a 10 year old. The divorcee's father threatened to murder should Harding was to marry his daughter. The daughter, whose name was Florence "Flossie" Mabel Kling DeWolf, was pursuing Harding until he caved in. Harding was 5 years younger than her.

Calvin Coolidge (1923-1929)

Coolidge is home to some very unique pets Two raccoons were given the names Rebecca Reuben and Rebecca. Reuben.

When he was eating breakfast at night, Coolidge would request someone to apply a head rub with petroleum jelly. It was believed that the jelly could protect his health.

Coolidge was constantly testing his staff using all the buttons on his desk before taking cover to watch them scurry to the office in fearful state. He then stepped out to inform them that they were checking the staff were actually working.

Herbert Hoover (1929-1933)

Hoover was adamant that he would not like to be seen by the staff in the White House, so he made them remain hidden from him whenever they passed by. If they refused to conceal, they could risk being fired from their job.

Being an orphan, Hoover was assigned to pick bugs from potatoes. To do this Hoover was paid $1.00 per 100 bugs he collected. Later in his life was when he began working in an underground mine.

He would use Chinese to talk privately with his wife.

Hoover's son was also a bit odd with his pet animals. He actually had two alligators as pets that frolicked through in the White House freely.

Hoover with his partner resided in the province of China in the time before the time of his presidency.

Franklin D. Roosevelt (1933-1945)

Thanks to the outstanding efforts of FDR He was awarded an honorary award with his portrait being placed on a coin following an act of Congress in 1945.

Roosevelt shared with a number of diners about an unsolved mystery Later, a journalist approached him to clarify the details of the story. It later became an actual film, and he received movie credits.

The President was the only one who served the presidency for more than two terms.

Roosevelt was obsessed with her dog that she would not let anyone else to eat her. The dog was named an official Army private in The 2nd World War. She was named Fala. The name made her popular with newspapers, and MGM created an animated comic strip featuring the dog and him. Two films which were made by MGM in connection with this story. Fala is immortalized as being the sole pet of her pet owner.

The wife of Roosevelt was not charged to change her name since it was Roosevelt too. In reality, they were cousins. They were escorted through the aisle with Theodore whom she identified as her Uncle as well as his cousin.

Roosevelt was as well closely related to Adams, Van Buren, Washington, Grant, Harrison, Madison, Taylor, Grant along with Winston Churchill.

Roosevelt was a believer in the supernatural and was not a fan of 13 as a number. Roosevelt would always have the number of guests 12-14 at the dinner parties and did not go on trips on the 13th of month.

Roosevelt had an illness that was rare, and was then believed as Polio. Recent research has proved that the illness was in fact Guillain-Barre Syndrome. It is a common occurrence within our society, yet was totally unknown in the past.

The Secret Service was told to take away the film footage of anyone who had taken photos of him sitting in his wheelchair. It wasn't widely known about his illness or even in the media.

Franklin was the fifth closest relative to Teddy Roosevelt.

Franklin flew in an aircraft to be an Presidential first.

Roosevelt had a meeting with the President Cleveland at the age of five years old. Cleveland said to Roosevelt that he wished for Roosevelt to not have to do the pressure of being President.

His appearance on TV took place during the 1932 World's Fair.

Chapter 3: Late 1900's Presidents Facts

Harry S. Truman (1945-1953)

The KKK has been taking over the policies of this nation for a long time. The moment Truman assumed his post and was urged to join the group. A lot of people have stated that it was introduced to him regardless of the fact that the KKK was not in existence in the moment. There are some who say that he joined the group of criminals but others claim that he didn't.

"S" in Harry S Truman is not a signification. This is the reason why there's no"S" in Harry S Truman, like it would for an alternative name.

He was a voracious reader. He was able to finish every single book available in the library in his town.

The very first bowling alley inside the White House was given to Truman to celebrate his birthday. The pin is displayed on the wall of the Smithsonian.

Truman married his wife at the age of six at Sunday school.

Truman employed as the term "haberdasher," which refers to the person who sells accessories for men, including hats. In 1921, Truman went insolvent as a haberdasher.

Truman is among the eight presidents who did not attend college.

Truman was a humble farmer who was from Missouri.

The first person in the 20th century to be without a degree from a university.

Dwight D. Eisenhower (1953-1961)

Eisenhower is more than an experienced war veteran, but also a President who was the only president who served during each of the World Wars.

At the time of his high school graduation, Eisenhower had an injured knee. The wound was so deep that it nearly required an amputation. The boy miraculously recovered.

Eisenhower was believed to have an relationship and Kay Summersby, who was his chauffeur during the war. Kay later wrote in a book about the tales of Eisenhower's inability to govern.

Ike served as the Allied Forces Commander during the 2nd World War.

Ike who was of the opinion that Shangri-La, the name originally used for Camp David, was too pretentious, therefore he altered the name in to Camp David.

He was a basic Kansas farmer.

Eisenhower was a golfer for over 800 hours of golf in his time as President.

He holds been awarded a Hall of Fame World Golf award in the category of Lifetime achievement.

Eisenhower disliked squirrels. He ensured that there were none in his White House lawn.

Eisenhower is the very first pilot to take a ride on an aircraft.

Eisenhower was a keen golfer too.

John F. Kennedy (1961-1963)

JFK is the most famous writer who wrote "Ask not what your country will do for you; instead, ask what you can do for your country" that means he is one of the presidents who advocate for helping others over your own interests. The President Warren G. Harding was one of the others with his famous speech during the Republican convention. He declared, "We need to be less concerned about what the government can do, and be more concerned about what the nation can do."

Kennedy was famous for his extramarital affairs were his while he was President. Some of his relationships were famous celebrities like Jay Mansfield, Angie Dickinson, Marilyn Monroe, Audrey Hepburn, Marlene Dietrich, as well as a stripper known as Star Blaze. However, that's not all. Kennedy also mingled with staffers of his White House, an airplane waitress, a few of his campaign staff as well as a handful of local secretariats, strippers and numerous other ladies who would like the man. In fact, there's an audio recording of the couple Inga Arvad as well as Kennedy having a romantic moment on an FBI videotape.

Kennedy did not receive a salary, and donated the money to charities.

Kennedy was a pioneer in many ways in his presidency:

* First Roman Catholic

* First Boy Scout

* First born at the turn of the century

Kennedy was born into a family with a lot of money. At the age of 21 the young man was given $1 million by his parents as a gift. The same thing happened to his siblings during their birthdays on the 21st of July as well.

Kennedy's dad wrote a letter to Harvard to admit him in which he said he's reckless and had no application. Although the praises were not great, he received a scholarship.

Kennedy loved James Bond movies. Even had the opportunity to meet the actor Ian Fleming. The event was an event in the 60s.

The group discussed possible solutions to Fidel Castro and ways to make him leave the office.

Lyndon B. Johnson (1963-1969)

Johnson took pride in his Harem. He set up a buzzer. The buzzer was installed for the express intention of alerting his office's entrance to security personnel. It was also used to serve to alert agents of the Secret Service to notify of the possibility that his wife would be coming to work.

Johnson was not sworn into office during an official ceremony, but instead in an aircraft. Johnson was the only person to be swear in by women.

Jackie Kennedy stood beside Johnson on the day that Johnson took the oath to ensure the security of the US. The blood was still on her clothes.

He earned his money prior to becoming President an auto mechanic and also a teacher.

Johnson utilized a ring bought that he purchased from Sears which cost $2.50 for his future spouse. Johnson also wrote her a total of 90 letters within the 90 days.

Johnson was known to ask his friends to follow him to the toilet. The purpose was to keep the conversation that they were engaging in.

Johnson was spared death when he went to the restroom in his time in the 2nd World War while waiting to take a plane off to fight. The plane was known as Wabash Cannonball and it crashed soon after take-off. Johnson had arrived late from the bathroom, and therefore missed his flight.

Johnson loved his own limb and christened the appendage Jumbo.

One reporter was constantly asking Johnson to explain why his soldiers were still being deployed to Vietnam and Johnson finally threw down his pants and exposed himself, and stated this as "why".

Johnson was 6'4" as well".

Richard Nixon (1969-1974)

Richard Milhous Nixon was the first president to travel to China as well as all 50 of US states. In addition, he was the only president to resign the presidency he was appointed to.

Nixon is among the top three known names of the populace in China together with Elvis Presley and Jesus Christ.

Nixon began playing poker so that he could play with his buddies for dollars. He won $6,000 playing an online game that financed Nixon's Presidential campaign.

Nixon talked to his Miami Dolphins coach and gave the coach a game to play at the Super Bowl VI.

Nixon introduced a single-lane bowling alley in the White House due to his obsession with bowling.

Nixon had a great understanding of playing five different instruments of music.

* Piano

* Accordion

* Clarinet

* Violin

* Saxophone

He was playing instruments, but he did not read sheet music.

Nixon participated of Watergate. Watergate scandal.

Gerald Ford (1974-1977)

Gerald Rudolph Ford was adopted but prior to his adoption the name he was given before adoption used to be Leslie Lynch King Jr.

While in the college years, Ford was a model and a forest ranger in Yellowstone. As an forest ranger, Ford fed bears, and control the flow of flow of traffic.

Ford served as the Vice Presidency for the first time in addition to the Presidency, without needing to be elected fully by the citizens. Ford was appointed ironically following Agnew's resignation. Agnew following which he was succeeding as the President following Nixon's resignation. Nixon.

Ford offered the school where he had his daughter's prom at the White House.

Two women, at different times within 17 days were attempting to kill Ford but failed.

Ford was model and was in the front cover of renowned magazine Cosmopolitan.

Ford played sports, and was a professional athlete and played Football at his school, the University of Michigan. Ford was a linebacker as well as an offensive center. He was offered spots on two different professional teams that he declined down.

Jimmy Carter (1977-1981)

The President who was the first to be born in an institution was Jimmy Carter.

The man was also the first person to see the first UFO. He did not reveal the sighting until several years later.

Carter was able to win his dream of winning the Nobel Peace Prize after he quit the presidency. Carter also constructed housing for people in need, and wrote 28 books.

Carter is the only president from the south who was elected post the end of the Civil War. This was a step towards restoring Davis to the US citizenship of Davis and also the presidency of the Confederate States.

A renowned peanut farmer located in Plains, Georgia, he was involved in an accident that led to his finger becoming permanently bent.

Carter appeared in the magazine Playboy. Carter wrote, "I have committed lust for women. I have committed the crime of adultery often in my heart. God will be able to forgive myself." He did not apologize for his unwise decision.

Ronald Reagan (1981-1989)

The University of California awarded the Most Nearly Perfect Male Profile award to Reagan in the year 1940.

Reagan is the very first president to be divorced.

Reagan was the longest-serving President to have served.

Reagan appeared as an act in stand-up comedy during Las Vegas for several weeks.

He was a believer in astrology and would consult an astrologer on regular basis. The astrologer he consulted was John Quigley. John Quigley would always consult with him before taking any decision or arranging the dates of any event .

He was almost naked in the art class which is sculpting human bodies.

Reagan was a star in films.

Reagan right after being shot by an assassin told reporters, "I forgot to duck."

George H.W. Bush (1989-1993)

Following the time that the presidency of President Bush Sr. became very sick, in front of the prime minister of Japan The Japanese developed one word that was new to the language spoken by the Japanese. The word Bushusuru refers to "doing the Bush thing," or vomiting out in the public.

When he was in working, a secret agents' children developed Leukemia Then Bush and the whole secret service shaved off their heads to show out of solidarity.

George H. W. Bush became President when he was elected in his vice presidency along with Martin Van Buren.

Bush was a great basketball player. He played forward for the team at his school. Also, he was the the captain of both team of baseball and soccer.

Bush Sr. is the only President elected with four different names.

Bush was the first President to have survived 4 crashes of planes in the 2nd World War.

Bush was struck by a bullet as he flew through Japan. The crewman and Bush had the luck of being able to jump out of the plane. The parachute used by the crewman did not work, and he crashed in the air with the plane. Bush was waiting for a lengthy time before being rescued after which he was eventually taken care of by the crew of a Navy submarine near the coast of Chichi-Jima.

Bush turned 90 years old with a jump from an aircraft. Bush jumped 6000 feet above the ground located in Kennebunkport, Maine.

Also, he had a birthday celebration with the same manner.

Chapter 4: Early 2000's President Facts

Bill Clinton (1993-2001)

First U.S. Democratic president William Jefferson "Bill" Clinton was the first to win reelection following Franklin D. Roosevelt.

Bill Clinton was a saxophone player and was a national television star.

Bill Clinton was the proud winner of two Grammy award.

Clinton had a great knowledge in the subject of My Little Pony. He was the winner of a bowl about it, and also won an award for the person who listened of the radio station Clinton was the host of.

Clintons features a perfectly symmetrical facial form that won her the respect of many women.

Clinton was a spoken-word artist who recorded two albums that he was awarded Grammys for.

He loves playing the saxophone often that he became a member of the band "3 blind mice." The band was active in the high school years.

George W. Bush (2001-2009)

G.W. Bush was a huge sports fan and possessed an extensive collection of baseballs. Over 250 in total.

At the high school He was head coach.

The President was the very was the first President and the only one to have kids who were twins.

Bush was believed to be closely related with Hugh Heffner. Heffner was also close with John Kerry.

His entire family had politics. His father was President and his brother Governor, as well as his grandpa from his father's family was a senator.

Bush was the sole President with a degree in the field of management.

Barack Obama (2009-2017)

He was the very first African American to run and later be the winner of the Presidential election not just once but two times.

Obama was a fan of nerds and enjoyed comics. He collected Conan the Barbarian and Spider-Man comics. He also has read Harry Potter. Harry Potter series.

Obama was a resident of Indonesia and also had an odd pet. It was an ape called Tata.

He worked for Baskin-Robbins in his teens and hated ice cream due to the taste of it.

The nickname was "O'bomber" in the high school basketball team because of his skills in basketball.

The applicant was invited to join an annual calendar featuring the best African American pinups, the all-girls committee was not happy with the application. It happened during his time at Harvard.

Barak Obama was awarded an Grammy for his performance as the voice of the reader from the story Dreams From My Father.

Obama's state of birth was Hawaii.

A ice cream shop located in Martha's Vineyard has an ice cream that is named in honor of Obama. It's called "Barack My World."

Chapter 5: Unusual Information about presidents

Six presidents were referred to as James:

Buchanan

Madison

Garfield

Monroe

Carter

Polk

Eastwood was at one time was the City Manager in Carmel, CA, was believed to be the Vice-President in the campaign of George Bush during the 1988 campaign.

Washington, Jackson, Monroe, Polk, Johnson, Taft, Harding, Roosevelt, McKinley, Buchanan, Garfield, F. Roosevelt, Johnson, Truman, and Ford were all part of the Free Masons. These could be the motives of the symbols depicted on the dollar note.

Jefferson owned a pet that was very unique and pets, grizzly bears to make precise. They lived in the White House in the front lawn.

Three of these presidents who left this world on the 4th of July.

Jefferson

Monroe

Adams

In a way, Coolidge was the president born on the 4th of July.

The sole person to have witnessed three Presidential assassins was Robert Lincoln, who is also the child of James Garfield. He was present at his father's murder, as well as McKinley's. Following his witnessing McKinley's murder McKinley's assassination, he pledged to never publicly interact with the President of the day.

Lincoln, Washington, Taylor, Van Buren, Johnson, Truman, Fillmore, Jackson and Cleveland weren't college students. Actually, none of them had a college degree. Truman was the only president during the 20th century who didn't have a university degree.

Each president was any child.

Madison, McKinley, and Cleveland are on the 500, $1000 dollars and the $5000-dollar bill. They aren't produced anymore. They are, however, in use as legal tender.

The president who gets a lot of attention has been John Hanson. Hanson was President from 1721 until 1783. It was before the union with the United States of America. He was a member of those days under the Articles of the Confederation. It was claimed by his family as well as many historians.

Three presidents got married during their time in office.

John Tyler, married Julia Gardiner in New York on June 26 1844. His wife's death 9 months prior.

In 1886, on June 2 Single Grover Cleveland got married to Frances Folsom at the White House.

Woodrow Wilson, who four months prior to the marriage of Cleveland got married to an individual called Edith Bolling Galt. They got married in the home of the bride's parents at Washington, D.C. The wedding was held on December 19, 1915, on the 18th day.

Mount Rushmore has four Presidential face carved into rock. The faces extend across the top of five stories. They measure 60 feet between the head and the face. Each pupil is four feet across. The mouths of every person is 18' in width. The process took 14 years to create them, and the price was $990,000. Between 1927 and 1941, they were able to remove 450,000 tons of stone which was lying on top of the mountain.

The wife of Roosevelt Eleanor Roosevelt took a flight together with Amelia Earhart. The flight took place across Washington D.C. and Baltimore.

Washington along with Madison were the two only presidents to have signed the constitution.

The website that was the first for the White House started on October 1994 while Clinton was President.

Theodore Roosevelt traveled out of the United States for business reasons being the first president to actually visit foreign territories. The location he aimed at was Panama which was scheduled to arrive on the that was 14 November 1906.

Lucy Webb Hayes was the first person to be awarded a degree from a university. It was her first female to graduate in 1850 Cincinnati of Wesleyan College who received a Liberal Arts degree.

Franklin D. Roosevelt flew across the ocean, becoming the first president to do this. In the beginning of January 1943, he flew at Port of Spain, Trinidad in Trinidad, and Belem from Miami and then Brazil to board Brazil for the Boeing 314 flying boat Bathurst in order to grow C-54 as well as Morocco.

British forces surrounded to the White House on 24th August 1814, prior to the fire which took place in the White House, during the conflict of 1812. Only one thing was salvaged, the Dolly Madison and

George Washington portraits created by Gilbert Stuart.

Supreme Court Chief Justice Thomas Todd was the officiant at the wedding ceremony in 1812 between Dolly Madison and Washington. It was the first time that a planned wedding ceremony held at the White House.

Woodrow Wilson while on the U.S.S. The ship was in the air through December 13, 1918, and 4, 1918. That made his the first president to travel across over the Atlantic Ocean to the Paris Peace Conference George Washington.

25th February 1828. 25th February 1828, President John Quincy Adams and his spouse resided within the White House with their lovely children.

Drinking alcohol was prohibited at every occasion in the Rutherford B. Hayes service duration. The result was a prohibition of "Lemonade Lucy" by the "First Lady Lucy Webb".

Abigail Fillmore, a former teacher at the school, was awarded money from the collective in 1850, which was used to construct the first library that was officially opened by the Mayor of Executive.

Eight presidents have died while during their term:

William Henry Harrison (1841, the onset of pneumonia)

James Garfield (1881, murder)

Franklin D. Roosevelt (1945, acute hemorrhage)

William McKinley (1901, murder)

Zachary Taylor (1850, acute)

Abraham Lincoln (1865, murder)

John F. Kennedy (1963, murder)

Warren G. Harding (1923, apoplexy)

Chester A. Arthur, Ulysses S. Grant, the president and Chester A. Arthur all had beards. Even though he also wore the mustache Cleveland wore unique parts.

In 1881, the President James Garfield in front of the White House from a special platform constructed for the for the opening parade was among the first presidents to be reviewed.

The President Ronald Reagan was the first president - between 1947 and 1952, as well as 1959-60 on Screen Actors Guild. Screen Actors Guild.

Franklin D. Roosevelt was the first president capable of having his mother cast a vote in the Presidential election.

Calvin Coolidge was able to request his father, notary of the public John Coolidge-to officiate his Presidential swearing-in ceremony on the 3 August 1923.

Woodrow Wilson had two daughters wedding at the White House during his Presidency: Jessie, November 25 1913, along and Francis B. Sayre, Sr. as well as Eleanor on May 7, 1914, along with Secretary of the Treasury, William G. McAdoo. Wilson was the only person to have this event happen.

James Garfield's mother was invited to be present at the inauguration. This was the first time a mother has been invited to go to an inauguration of the president.

George W. Bush completed the marathon. He ran his Marathon in Houston in 3 hours 44 minutes and 52 secs on the morning of January 24 1993. The first President to participate in at a marathon.

Chapter 6: From Missouri to the White House

Harry S. Truman was appointed to Truman's Oval Office on April 12 1944. Three months prior to that, Truman had been a part of the United States Senate, one of the ninety-six people who were part of the organization. He was the youngest senator of Missouri which indicated his inexperience within the chamber. Truman was selected as a running mate in compromise to Franklin Delano Roosevelt at the Democratic National Convention in July of 1944, Truman campaigned with the president for a record-breaking fourth term. Because of Roosevelt's health issues the fact was in the Washington the political elite that Truman might be asked to become the president of the United States. However, not many believed Truman would be the country's chief executive in just three months in office as the 30th vice president of the United States. The Roosevelt-Truman team easily defeated their Republican adversaries governor Thomas Dewey of New York and Senator John Bricker of Ohio, during the 1944 Presidential election. They won the election mostly because of Roosevelt's massive popularity the majority of Americans were unaware of Roosevelt, who would eventually become the country's thirty-third president.

Harry Truman was an improbable president who was a bit of a stretch. Truman did not display any impressive charisma or charm and he had a normal background which contrasted starkly with Roosevelt. Roosevelt who been a student at various universities for a long time. Truman did not pursue an education beyond the secondary level or professional training, and his sole non-political background was serving working in the military, farming as well as running a variety of small and unsuccessful enterprises. Truman was, in fact, Truman was the first President after Grover Cleveland who had not had a degree from a college or university. But, Truman was a quiet person who was regarded for being a smart scholar as well as a devoted history buff an ardent worker, and a reliable all-around friend. Truman was continuously striving to achieve the awe-inspiring stature and luster of the late President Roosevelt who was perhaps the most successful president of the 20th century.

Harry Truman came from Independence, Missouri, a small town that was not far away from Kansas City, although he was born in Lamar. The parents of his father, John Anderson Truman and Martha Ellen Young, had three children. Their most senior Harry. Harry Truman, born on May 8th, 1884.

An enthusiastic student who had impressive abilities on the piano Truman was a clerical and service worker for a variety of clerical and service jobs when he graduated from high school. then returning to the rural area of Missouri to work on the farm up until America entered during the First World War. As he was preparing for his deployment in France, Truman met Eddie Jacobson as well as James Prendergast, both of who had an impact on his professional and political future. With a distinguished career during the war, including serving as a captain and lieutenant, Truman returned home to Independence and married Bess Wallace. The couple had one baby, who was named Margaret.

Truman's wartime connections were vital when he entered the political arena. He was elected in 1922 to the position of judge on the county court with assistance from Tom Prendergast, the head of the famous Prendergast Democratic party. Prendergast was the father of Truman's best friend James Prendergast from his military times It was James who brought Truman and Prendergast to communicate with each other. Truman was unable to hold the post at the time of the 1924 Republican wave that led to the return of the President Calvin Coolidge of Massachusetts. In 1926, however Truman was elected the county's chief judge in charge of overseeing and assisting many infrastructure initiatives all over Jackson County.

Although Truman enjoyed a great results in local politics but he'd always wanted to pursue a career in Washington. Before the 1934 midterm elections Truman would like to get the nomination of the Democratic Party to take on current Republican Senate Roscoe Patterson. Tom Prendergast, however, was skeptical of Truman's capability to compete in the Senate on Capitol Hill, and sought for another candidate to back. However, when Prendergast was unable to locate a suitable candidate and he opted to vote for Truman and he won both his primary and general election, beating senator Roscoe Patterson by a massive margin. Truman was able to defeat his Republican adversaries by a margin of more than 200 thousands votes.

At the time that Truman came to Washington there was a misconception that he, as the majority of his predecessors was just one of the foot soldiers for the family of Prendergast in Congress. But Truman determinedly proved the people wrong. He would often rail against the powerful corporations. This was a topic that he often returned to in his time at the White House. The emergence of Truman to the limelight occurred during the planning for America's war efforts in the first stages in the Second World War. Following numerous instances of abuses of government funds used for military use, Truman called for the establishment of a specialized Senate committee that would investigate the military program of the United States. It was established in 1941, it was to be referred to as Truman Committee. Truman Committee, named after the chairman of the committee's proceedings. It would eventually lead the inquiry. In the end, it was suggested that the Truman Committee found up to 15 billion in wasted and misused funds that were allocated to military spending by the federal government. its recommendations spared American taxpayers from paying a huge amount. Time Magazine would call the Truman Committee one of the top government departments during that time period of that Second World War.

It was the accomplishment Truman enjoyed in leading his committee of special interest that brought him into the limelight and eventually earned Truman a spot in the Democratic ticket helmed by Roosevelt. Roosevelt in 1944's Presidential election. The Vice President of Roosevelt in his final term was Henry Wallace, the son of an ex- Republican Secretary of Agriculture however, many believed that he was too liberal for the position of President if Roosevelt's passing. Then, with Roosevelt intent on selecting one of Truman as well as Supreme Court Justice William Douglas for his running mate and having the majority of his voters expressing their preference to Truman as their choice, the Senator from Missouri was chosen as the candidate of the Republican Party as Vice President.

Even though the Democratic ticket was a clear winner during October 1944's

Presidential election however, many Americans were only aware of Truman as a member of his committee, the Truman Committee, and he became a rather unnoticed person. When he was sworn into office by the Vice Presidency on the 20th of January in 1945 Truman wasn't often contacted by Roosevelt and was largely left out of all policy-making decisions.

In the event that Roosevelt died on the 12th of April 1945 Truman served as Vice President for just eighty-two days. He had very little understanding of the complexities of the presidency or America's efforts to fight. But, Truman was called on to be the President of the United States through a period of turmoil and met the task head-on. Truman discovered the news of Roosevelt's death upon being summoned by his White House following an afternoon of presidency over a session of the Senate. Roosevelt's wife Eleanor who informed him of the information.

The passing of Roosevelt's wife would have major impact on the course of Second World War. The Japanese imperialists viewed the death as a significant chance to win, and chose to fight untested politicians instead of a seasoned statesman. In the home country, the entire nation was in a trance. A lot of people mourned the loss of the longest-serving President in America but were also anxious about the possibility that Truman was, being a man with such a small size would be the successor. The eyes of the world's observers were focused on Washington as Truman was sworn into the presidency at around 7pm at the Cabinet room in the White House. With Bess close by with their daughter Margaret in the background, Harry Truman took the Presidential swearing-in ceremony to be the 30th President of the United States, simultaneously becoming probably the most powerful individual on earth.

Following the inauguration ceremony, which was conducted to the Cabinet by the Chief Justice Harlan Stone in the Cabinet room, Truman assembled Roosevelt's Cabinet. Truman assured his Cabinet that the administration would be able to continue implementing Roosevelt's plan, and the plan was to accomplish this by involving the whole Cabinet. The first thing he did as President was to give instructions authorities to ensure his United Nations founding meeting in San Francisco went ahead as scheduled. Being the first President to serve as a member of the United States Senate since Warren G. Harding's demise in 1923 Truman was able to benefit from his strong connections to Congress however, he was hindered by the image of the institution. It was the general pattern throughout the 20th century was appointment of Governors who had served before to the presidency, with notables like Franklin Roosevelt, Woodrow Wilson and Theodore Roosevelt having all served as Chief Executives in their states of residence. His presidency was somewhat controversial, but Truman had to face the responsibility of dealing with the legacy of his predecessor.

Many people were worried about Truman's ascendance to the presidency, some believed in Truman's capabilities as a President. John Nance Garner, who was Roosevelt's first Vice President over eight years was awed by Truman as a man with confidence and conviction. And even Republicans like Arthur Vandenberg, one of the most powerful senators in the Senate in the era believed Truman as being able to handle the challenge. Vandenberg himself stated that Truman was a man of "high honesty of purpose," one who was able to take on the leadership of America in a war. Although many initially were worried about Truman as the first American to undergo a leader to change over 12 years, many were later to realize the fact that Roosevelt did a great choice when he chose to nominate the successor to his own.

Much like his adversaries, Truman was quite solemn regarding his quick climb to the Presidency. He was worried about his lack of knowledge and of the challenge in succeeding to a person who had the same stature as Franklin Roosevelt as well as someone who was acknowledged for being one of the globe's many big names throughout the 20th century. Truman later said in a press conference after visiting Capitol Hill, Truman felt "like the moon, the stars, and all the planets had fallen on me."

In his very first day as a president, Truman was fully briefed on the status of the American military effort as well as the current situation in Europe. Secretary of State Stettinius explained the stark divisions becoming apparent between Americans as well as the Soviet allies. The Secretary of State Stettinius, however, noted that Truman was not active in the field of foreign affairs, nor was he a meeting with any of the other world leaders such as all the Allied nations. But, Truman, like President Roosevelt earlier was given important summaries of key issues that occurred across the globe every day, that helped the newly elected President get acquainted with the present world situation. The President also demanded from Secretary Stettinius to provide an overview of the main issues facing America. United States in every region in the world. In the briefing, it was suggested that Britain's foreign policy is primarily based on maintaining an enduring relation with its American partner, and recommended to the American administration do everything can to assist France recover. In a declaration that was intended to hint at the challenges to come in the future, the Truman briefing stated the fact that "the Soviet Government has taken a firm and uncompromising position on nearly every major question that has arisen in our relations." Concerning relations in Germany with its Nazi regime in the briefing, the State Department outlined American policy objectives, which included that of "destruction of National Socialist organizations and influence, punishment of war criminals, [and] disbandment of the Germany military establishment." Areas that were liberated of Europe will also need to have access to essential items for the people of the region. Restoring their spirits will be the only means to ensure stability in the political system and help reestablish the democratic government that was overthrown. A few other minor goals were also covered in the presentation. After his very first day as President Truman realized that he was left with many things to master in terms of comprehending the complexities of American foreign policy.

As the military advisors of President Obama were gathered inside the Oval Office for their first formal meeting with the newly elected President, they spoke candidly about the situation of battle across Europe as well as Asia. The group comprised the Secretary of War Henry Stimson, Secretary of the Navy James Forrestal, Army Chief of Staff George Marshall, Chief of Naval Operations Ernest King, Commander of the Air Force Barney Giles, and President's Chief of Staff, William Leahy. They all predicted the Nazis were not going to be defeated for six more months or longer in the future, and Japan will be able to endure for over an entire year and half. All participants convened that no action or significant decisions could be taken until after President Truman made his appearance before Congress. When the military advisors of President Truman were leaving in the Oval Office, Truman asked Leahy to remain behind and also asked that he stay in the position of principal assistant to Truman. Leahy was happy to accept.

The President Truman was also able to decide during his first day in office, who he wanted to nominate as his Secretary of State. Edward Stettinius had already indicated that he wanted to leave the job and Truman would like to choose James Byrnes, President Roosevelt's Director of the Office of War Mobilization, to succeed him. Byrnes was invited to the White

House and was informed by President Truman that he was likely to designate him Secretary of State when the United Nations conference in San Francisco concluded in within a couple of weeks. Truman was interested in Byrnes as Secretary of his State Department for his valuable knowledge, as well as his experience in politics. With no Vice President, Truman's Secretary of State could be next on the list for President should something happen to the President. Therefore, he sought to have a Secretary of State that was experienced in the field of politics. Something that Stettinius evidently did not have. Byrnes was a former elected member of both the House, Senate, and an Associate Justice of the Supreme Court, so he surely had the qualifications to take over the presidency. In 1947 under the leadership of Truman, Congress would approve the Presidential Succession Act in 1947, which would place

The Speaker of the House of Representatives, a popular elected official, as the next in line to become the next President following The Vice-President. Truman was concerned after his election over the potential dangers posed by his 1886 Presidential Succession Act, which was a law that placed Secretary of State as the second on the list of candidates for the presidency.

On the 14th of April 1945, the date of Roosevelt's funeral, Truman received two cables from the prime minister Churchill from Great Britain, who informed Truman about the possibility that the Soviet army in east moving west and those of the American and British army in the west, marching to the east, were scheduled to be meeting in the coming weeks at Eastern Germany. Churchill advised that Truman, Truman, and Stalin each release an announcement about the upcoming event and that it could be beneficial to all people around the globe that would feel secure with an Allied triumph in Europe. Truman accepted the suggestion, with Stalin's acceptance. Churchill further informed Truman that despite the plans that were made under the Roosevelt administration however, a few of the bombardment operations planned for the German industrial zones weren't necessary anymore in the sense that any reaction might further threaten London. London. After conferring and negotiating with Joint Chiefs, agreed with Churchill in this regard also.

The funeral of Roosevelt was scheduled for the afternoon of The new President took an insignificant part of the service, because the wife of Mrs. Roosevelt had requested that there would be no eulogies in the ceremony. Truman, Bess and Margaret Truman, Bess, and Margaret followed the Roosevelt family in the train New York, where Franklin Roosevelt was laid to rest the next morning. Truman was on his way back to Washington in the afternoon was at the train station setting the final touches to his speech that he would give to Congress in the next day.

Following a period of grief, Truman set out to leave his mark on American policy with his remarks to Congress on the 16th of April, just four days after having been elected President. The previous day, Truman was informed by Stalin within his Soviet Union that he would be willing to have an official statement jointly released to proclaim the end of Germany. The rather optimistic developments of Europe, Truman met with British Foreign Secretary Anthony Eden before departing for Congress to deliver his address.

In the morning, when Truman was on Capitol Hill, he was received by his former colleagues and fellow senators who had served at the Senate which it was he left just three months prior. The senator waited outside Speaker Sam Rayburn's office and had a conversation with Congressional representatives before departing for the House to address the country at 1 o'clock at the end of the day. As Truman arrived in his first session in the House of Representatives, he received a roaring applause. The judges from the Supreme Court had even ensured that they would be present during Truman's address.

When he began his inaugural speech to Congress as well as the American citizens as their commander in chief Truman, President Truman stated in clear terms that he was going to take the steps of his administration the manner that Roosevelt would have liked for him to. He committed to carrying his ideals of the previous

President forward. Truman was able to speak clearly and uncompromisingly in protection of freedom throughout the world in a pledge to protect freedom's cause by all his force and power.

As Roosevelt, Truman demanded an unconditional surrender as his only way to end the Second World War, and stressed the need for the United Nations as a means to maintain peace in the wake of the current war. America was, as he stated, should not repeat the errors made in the aftermath of the First World War, in where the nation reverted to an isolationist mindset in the expectation of being secure within its border. The dream of security was destroyed by the events of Pearl Harbor, and Truman wanted to make sure that the idea of isolation would never be a part of United States foreign policy. Furthermore, he distinguished participation from interference. He said that any state seeking to be a good one seeks to help others, not be a dictatorship and he emphasized this throughout his presidency.

In the wake of receiving almost universal approval for his speech before Congress, Truman found that his speech received the approval even if it was temporary, of both political parties in Congress. They aimed to assist the transition process into becoming the White House, and even his Republican allies from the Senate truly wished him well and each spoke of his warm and friendly fellow who was a member of them for only a few months prior to.

Truman took a number of important decisions within his first couple of weeks in office. He named Charlie Ross, a boyhood acquaintance, journalist as well as a Pulitzer Prize recipient, as his press secretary. He demanded that he be present at 8am early, instead of waiting until 10 am to get there just like Roosevelt did. Additionally, as opposed to Roosevelt, Truman refused to make use of J. Edgar Hoover's FBI to gather details for purposes of politics. Truman and Hoover would grow to be bitterly resentful of one another and Truman insisting he would be the sole one to contact the FBI via the Attorney General's office. Truman even compared the FBI and the actions of Hoover with the actions of the secret police. Truman was not interested in the use of blackmail or information that was scandalous and he was astonished by the actions of Hoover. Truman was also greeted by a group of members of the Senate Republican caucus the 18th of April, nearly every member of the group had never visited the White House since the Hoover administration was in place, since Roosevelt was unable to invite them into the White House. After having a number of visitors and officials in the

White House over the following couple of days Truman was finally beginning to sense that the President was becoming more aware about the obligations and responsibilities associated with the presidency.

Truman engaged in extensive discussions also with W. Averell Harriman, the United States Ambassador to the Soviet Union, who landed in Washington on the 20th of April. He was Harriman that was assigned the responsibility of educating Truman with the current situation in Russia. Harriman pointed out that Stalin was pursuing two main goals in mind: to work to the United States and Great Britain as well as gain greater influence and control within Eastern Europe. According to Harriman quickly pointed that these two goals were in conflict with one another. When concerns over and the Soviet Union began to deepen within Washington,

Truman pledged to adopt a fair, but firm approach to the bilateral relationship. Some, like Harriman were concerned the ally of America's indefinitely known as that of the Soviet Union, could prove to be a more enemy of totalitarianism than the Nazis and the imperialist Japan. In fact, Roosevelt was beginning to recognize the fact that Stalin was not a reliable ally.

His arguments could hint at the Truman administration's perspective on the start in the Cold War. According to Harriman claimed that his argument was that the Soviet Union could not be relied upon. They wanted to control Eastern Europe through a "barbarian invasion" as well as ignore established rules of international relations. This was what Stalin was doing in Poland through the establishment of a new government which would follow orders from Moscow even though that the Soviets declared, and said, they would do otherwise. If the current trend within Poland remain, Truman was certain that the Senate could not ever agree to approve a treaty that would establish the United Nations. However, Harriman was certain of the possibility that there was a chance that the Soviet Union could be negotiated in conjunction with.

President Truman was first given a thorough review of the nation's financial situation after a meeting the Treasury Secretary Henry Morgenthau on April 20. Morgenthau said that the federal government's expenses for budget year 1944-5 exceeded than twice the amount it earned. As a whole, the expenses totalled up to $99 billion. the majority of it was allocated to wartime expenditures. The revenue was only $4 billion, but Morgenthau was keen to launch an expansive campaign against tax avoidance. In addition to domestic costs, Allied nations from around the globe were asking the American Treasury to help. China demanded more gold in order to lower inflation. The British will require assistance after the conflict, France wanted funds to aid in reconstruction and India is asking for help also. In the end, Treasury Department would clearly have many demanding days over the weeks to come. The good news occurred on the 21st of April after the President was told about the German resistance was breaking down across Europe as Allied troops were quickly moving towards the center of Nazi the territory.

On the 22nd of April, 9 days following Truman was inaugurated, Soviet Foreign Minister Vyacheslav Molotov made a formal trip to Washington in his journey towards San Francisco to participate in negotiations to create of the United Nations. It was the presence of Molotov himself was present was crucial: Stalin had long intended to invite an unofficial junior to attend the United Nations meeting to play down the significance of the group. But, ambassador Harriman had managed convince Stalin to invite Molotov in a gesture of kindness following the passing of the president Roosevelt.

The most contentious issue was Poland. The Soviets wanted to install the country with a Moscow friendly administration within this Eastern European country regardless of prior commitments to open and democratic elections. Furthermore the way in which the Soviet Union reacted towards the crisis in Poland quickly became a an integral part of a larger trend. The Russians seemed to be expanding towards a variety of Eastern European nations, most particularly Romania. Their earlier commitments to the Yalta Conference in favor of open elections did not seem to seem to be worth the paper it was printed on. Truman and his staff members agreed that Washington had to cooperate in the face of Soviet Union. However, one of the main concerns was to make sure that the partnership among America and Russia remains intact to allow Russia to join in the battle against Japan.

Truman did not mince words when he spoke to Molotov. Truman suggested that Truman said that the United States would not recognize any government from Poland which was not elected through a fair election. Molotov was directed to inform Stalin his that Stalin that the United States expected the Soviet government to live up to the promises they made previously. Truman was adamant that the United States was honoring its obligations that the president Roosevelt at his meeting in Yalta with Winston Churchill and Joseph Stalin in Yalta as well as Truman believed that Russia to honor the same. Truman's frustration and determination towards the Soviet government will only increase over the years and months in the years ahead.

On the 23rd of April one day following Molotov's visit, Truman was able to meet with close advisers inside his Oval Office to discuss the consequences of his previous discussions. Foreign ministers from Great Britain, Russia and the United States had met earlier this morning. The Secretary of State said that the Russians seemed to be determined to violate the deal reached in Yalta for open and democratic election in Poland. According to what President Truman stated to his advisors just those from the United States and Great Britain appeared to have abided by the agreement signed by three of the leaders. Even though they have made a significant contributions to the war effort across Europe and the Middle East, the Soviets were not regarded to be a true all-weather ally.

Truman was in contact with Molotov at a later time in the afternoon. Truman emphasized to Molotov the Soviet foreign minister that Truman believed that the United States could not allow the establishment of a regime put in Poland that didn't represent the interests of all the citizens of Poland. Truman also stated in his speech that his United States would go forward by promoting the establishment of the United Nations regardless of the situation of American relations with Russian relations. Truman also stated that President Truman sent Molotov an email to send to Stalin which described the potential for conflict between all three Allied nations.

The President Truman was briefed in full on Truman's involvement with the Manhattan Project for the first occasion on the 25th of April. The meeting was conducted by Henry Stimson, Roosevelt's Secretary of War. He was a long-standing Republican politician, as well as a notable public service. Stimson was also as Secretary of War thirty years earlier under the presidency of William Howard Taft, and was the Secretary of State for Herbert Hoover. At a conference in the Oval Office attended only by the Secretary of War General Leslie Groves, who was responsible for the Manhattan Project, and the President himself Stimson told Truman that Truman was told that the United States would have a nuclear bomb on its hands within four months' time. He also said that this weapon was the most lethal weapon ever created through the ages of humankind. Stimson also warned that Russia would likely be working to develop comparable capabilities. The decision of the United States to explore development of a nuclear weapon came from the anticipation of the possibility that Nazi Germany could acquire nuclear weapons, but they did not come even close to assembling a complete weapon. The nuclear arsenal would offer America United States with a means to bring about a quicker ending to the war and saving hundreds of American lives along the way.

After a brief meeting together with Stinson along with Groves, Truman departed for the Pentagon to reach out to British the Prime Minister Winston Churchill. They discussed an espionage invitation made by Nazis that were seeking at pursuing some type of discussions. Heinrich Himmler had suggested that although Germany is willing to work to the Western alliance, it was not interested in the notion of surrendering to Soviets. The possibility of a German surrender could also mean freedom for Italy, Norway, Denmark, Yugoslavia, and Holland five nations which were occupied and were located to the in the west of Germany. Both Truman as well as Churchill considered that Nazis were required to hand over to the three countries all at once. They were willing to inform Joseph Stalin of the communication and the conclusion.

While American as well as British forces in west, as well as Soviet forces from the east were racing towards Germany there were disagreements over the boundaries of occupational zones quickly arose. Three powers initially reached an agreement on occupational zones which were laid out in London at the beginning of January in this year. As the army began to march toward Berlin the precise boundaries would not be able to be maintained and the plans for occupation would need been adjusted in order to reflect the actual situation in the field. In the end, it was suggested by the British government, as well as Truman administration, Truman administration, suggested the borders previously negotiated are to be reinstated in the event that the circumstances in the battlefield would permit armies to allow it. Communication between the three largest powerhouses should continue in a continuous manner. A few weeks before his demise in 1939, President Roosevelt issued a decree concerning the treatment of insecure Germany. He chose that General Eisenhower was to serve as a governor of the military in the American-occupied territories, however a civilian could be named High Commissioner for Germany during the next few months. The Truman's advisers were also worried about the potential for mass hunger and homeless. Great Britain and other Allied countries were suffering massive food shortages, too. The President ordered that measures be taken to assist our wartime ally nations during their current food shortage crisis.

There was a growing tension among the Allied leadership on Poland was evident by the end of April. On the 29th of April, Premier Churchill issued a letter to Stalin expresses his displeasure at the Soviet president's inability to adhere in accordance with the Yalta accords. The Yalta agreements stipulated that Poland would be unified and independent, and that its administration should not be subordinate to an outside power. However, Stalin who was enraged at the fact that Truman and Churchill were seeking to make Soviet the policy of Poland even though Poland was Russia's closest neighbor, was not ready to engage in discussions. With his telegram for the

Russian partner, Churchill foreshadowed the dark possible scenario of a globe divided in two parts.

The pace of change within Europe have been rapid in Europe. Italy's dictator of the fascist kind, Benito Mussolini, was murdered by rebels on the 28th of April. The Nazi force in Italy officially gave up its arms at the hands of Allied forces on the 29th of April. Since there weren't Soviet forces present in Italy, Nazi leaders were more hesitant to give up their positions for Allied forces than elsewhere, citing fears of Communist brutality that was bound to come with Russian forces. Their fears over the surrender to Soviet forces in other countries were confirmed to be right. Truman utilized the declaration that he made following his surrender to Axis force in Italy to inform Germany as well as Japan that only unconditional surrender would protect them from complete destruction.

Hitler killed himself on April 30 The following day, Berlin was taken under the control and protection of the Allies in May 2. It was that day, May 7, one week following the time that Adolf Hitler had killed himself the day that Germany completely and without reservation handed over to Allied forces. Despite the fact that Truman permitted Stalin to hold off making the official announcement until next day. It was the Western Allies had received messages weeks earlier indicating that Nazi forces were willing to surrender rather than the Russians However, Truman and Churchill were concerned about the conflict that could arise if Nazis do not give up the three Allies at once that was finally done on the 7th of May. On May 8 1945 the President Truman and the Prime Minister Churchill and Comrade Stalin each announced unconditional surrender, which was accepted by the German Army. The newly elected American President characterized the moment in terms of "a solemn but glorious hour." Following just a few days in the office of President, Harry Truman had presided over the end of the conflict in the European front. The last and formal German authority surrender accord was signed by Allied leaders on June 5th, transferring control of the country to the four superpowers.

Even though the war was over, conflict in Europe as a whole, the American military effort was very active. Although the Germans as well as their Nazi allies in Europe were laying down their weapons, Japan was still committed to fighting its allies, the United States and its allies. Even as the president Truman immediately urged Japan to give up its arms along with other Axis forces but the Japanese leaders resisted to consider the suggestion. Truman took aim at the Japanese management during an open press conference in order to affirm the Nazis have surrendered. Truman released a similar declaration the following day, in his broadcast address to the country.

As the conflict in Europe ended, a large portion of across Europe and the United States immediately turned their focus toward Japan. However, Truman was not done with the European situation as was his counterpart of Great Britain. Churchill advised Truman prior to Germany's surrender to ensure that he had a robust presence throughout Eastern Europe, apprehensive of the possibility that a retreat that was imposed by the United States might allow for the Soviet Union to swallow up areas of the eastern region of Europe. Truman further stated that to Churchill that he would insist to oblige to force the Soviet Union to adhere to the boundaries agreed upon at the 1944 Quebec Conference and finalized at Yalta.

However, Churchill remained very concerned about the European scenario, assuming that Stalin will do whatever possible to extend Soviet territories to Europe This is the reason the reason why Prime Minister Truman repeatedly urged Roosevelt as well as Truman to see Truman and Roosevelt have Western Allied forces push as to the east as they could before the war was brought to its conclusion.

Though he had hoped to ensure that Roosevelt's Cabinet roughly in place, Truman made several changes during his first few months of office. The Senator Lewis Schwellenbach was appointed to succeed Frances Perkins as Secretary of Labor as well as Tom Clark of Texas was selected to succeed Francis Biddle as Attorney General. Secretary of State nominees were also selected to positions such as the Postmaster General as well as

Agriculture. The Postmaster General of the new administration would be Robert Hannegan, the Chairman of the Democratic National Committee, while Clinton Anderson was installed in the Agriculture Department. Truman was already deciding to appoint Jimmy Byrnes as Secretary of State. He got his confirmation from the Senate in the early part of July. When reorganizing the composition of his Cabinet, Truman had chosen to select faithful Democrats Many of them were members of Congress. It was a further initiative by Truman's administration to rebuild relations between the legislative and executive branches.

A different personnel decision Truman did shortly following the conclusion of the conflict in Europe was to prove an more radical departure from the Roosevelt style than the Cabinet reforms. Herbert Hoover, the only Former President still living, was asked to visit Truman in his White House. Hoover was a target of Roosevelt who was constantly seeking to undermine his image. However, Truman thought that Hoover was extremely useful in managing the epidemic of famine throughout Europe due to his experience following his experiences during the First World War. Hoover was happy to be in any way he could to help the president and all those who were suffering in Europe He readily agreed with Truman's suggestion that he assist with the relief of food which would be desperately needed by America's allies over the months ahead.

As Truman did not stop settling to his new White House, America was more than ever close to finalizing building the first nuclear weapon in the world. The group that was charged with overseeing development of the technology was led by Henry Stimson, the Secretary of War. Truman was also appointing his upcoming to become Secretary of State Jimmy Byrnes, as his personal representative in the civilian authority. The panel agreed to three key principles late in May. It was first decided that nuclear weapons should be employed against Japan whenever possible with the intention of swiftly ending the war, and also avoiding the cost of a ground incursion. Then, the eight people participating in the debates agreed that nuclear weapons is to be used with no prior warning. Additionally, it must be dropped over the area that could cause the greatest psychological harm to the Japanese citizens, and this could result in thousands of civilian victims. Although none of the members in the committee were certain about the extent of harm the nuclear weapon might cause however, they were all certain the consequences would be devastating.

In the midst of war, Japan progressed and Japan fought on, Japanese forces continued to wage war, and the United States air force continued to bombard Japanese areas at an alarming pace. With Japanese believing in the necessity to fight until the final, many believed the use of nuclear weapon was necessary. However, Secretary Stimson and others was concerned that due to the numerous bombings that have already taken place all over the world as well as the fact that it was likely that the United States would find it difficult to find an area in Japan that would allow the nuclear weapon to display its maximum capability. Furthermore, such a goal was vital since Truman as well as Stimson believed that Japan's Japanese Emperor, as well as associates will only be willing to give up their power when confronted with such an extreme degree of destruction.

Despite Churchill's warnings to the contrary, the Truman administration decided to draw American forces out of Soviet zone of occupation to ensure it was the United States adhered to the agreements reached at Yalta. Truman was officially announced to Churchill that America was withdrawing of the Russian zones on the 21st of June and that the procedure was scheduled to start immediately. However, there were signs suggesting that the Soviets did not intend of delivering on the promises they made at that exact same conference. While no decisions had been taken regarding the destiny of Poland and what would happen to Eastern Europe, the three Allied leaders decided to gather to discuss the future of Eastern Europe in Potsdam, Germany on July 15th. Truman wanted to keep the peace between the so-called Three Powers throughout the war.

While combat in Europe was over however, there was still a long way to go. Second World War was by not over. Yet, many members of Congress wanted to end the financial assistance to Allied nations that were desperately in need of help. Concerns were growing throughout Europe, Truman released a clarifying statement that eased anxieties among the allies of America, declaring that there wouldn't necessarily be an end to the wartime support for monetary aid. In an open letter addressed to the speaker of the House of Representatives, "the war against Japan, like the war against Germany, is a cooperative Allied effort ...[therefore] we shall continue to pool our resources with those of our allies."

Meanwhile, the efforts were underway to prepare to launch a ground attack on Japan. The question was not determined if Japan or the United States would simply drop an nuclear bomb on Japan or begin a large-scale ground attack. However, Truman's advisers cautioned that a military attack on Okinawa will be extremely expensive. General MacArthur's advisers set their estimates of casualties for the initial 30 days as fifty thousand, an astounding amount which would surpass the loss of life during the Battle of Normandy in France in the previous year. In the event that the Pentagon added other regions which could be attacked in the same manner as Okinawa as part of their estimate and the number of casualties expected surpassed 200 and fifty thousand. Secretary Stimson was concerned that the Japanese were likely to continue fighting to the end which could mean at least 1 million American troops would lose their lives before the Japanese had been defeated. In the plans of the invasion, it was stated that the mission was to begin in November 1945, and continue until 1946. They were accepted by Truman before his departure to San Francisco to make a speech on the 26th of June. But, American's plans to invade might change rapidly based on whether or it was it was the case that Soviet Union made a commitment to declare war against Japan.

The future of China and China's future. Chinese were not able to remain in China for long. Chinese participated in the war by sides with the Allies and were being encircled and abused by Japanese troops. Truman took a long time working with his advisers as well as Stalin to come up with a compromise regarding the future of the Chinese allies. In the end, Truman, Stalin, and Churchill each agreed that the Chinese anti-Japanese force that were commanded by general Chiang Kai-shek, should be appointed to the new administration and be given the necessary tools to unite China after an eventual Japanese withdraw. In spite of their pledge to back Chiang and his forces, it would be the Soviets who were responsible to undermine Chiang's Nationalist government during the following years due to their support for Mao Zedong's Communists. The deal between the top heads also specified it was the United States, Great Britain and China, the Soviet Union, and China were granted a administration over Korea and China, a different area that will later result in conflict between the Soviets as well as their present Western allies.

Chapter 7: Winning the War

As Harry Truman arrived in Europe and saw the entire severity of the destruction which was now afflicting Germany. The roads, cities and factories were ruined. Many were left without homes or food. The spread of disease and death was a constant. When he travelled for Potsdam for Potsdam Conference, Truman was in the company of a huge group comprising representatives of his administration. The delegation included the Secretary of State as well as Truman, the American ambassador to his country, the Soviet Union. Chefs, doctors and even a chauffeur were included too.

Three leaders would all stay at Babelsberg which was a tiny town located outside Potsdam. It was guarded with Soviet, American and British troops to protect Stalin, Truman, and Churchill. Truman's objective was to solve certain issues which remained unresolved in the aftereffects from the Yalta Conference and to get acquainted with his colleagues. Leaders would discuss about the state of affairs of Eastern Europe and Russia's contribution to the conflict against Japan. This was the issue which Truman was most keen to address. Truman was meticulously preparing for this meeting over the course of several weeks, dedicating dozens of hours with his closest international policy advisers. Truman wanted to guarantee that the influence of his country United States in world affairs particularly in the event the prospect of replacing a notable president as Franklin Roosevelt.

Truman first had a meeting with Winston Churchill on July 16. He was a seasoned politician, and a strong head in the British Empire during his time in the Second World War, Churchill as well as Roosevelt was extremely acquainted in dealing with

Joseph Stalin, and with the dealings with foreign leaders on an individual basis. This was all something new to Truman. Maybe because he was armed with a vast amount of experience dealing internationally-related political issues. Churchill did not prepare for the meeting as thoroughly as Truman had done, neither was his group larger. The two leaders were meeting to the first time Churchill was accompanied with his foreign secretary Anthony Eden, and his Permanent Under Secretary Alexander Cadogan.

While Churchill was a seasoned global leader, he facing a insolvent Empire as well as personal fatigue. More important, however, is that of the British general election that was held on July 5but the outcome would not be available for another few weeks, until the votes cast by soldiers were taken into account. While few people anticipated that at the time,

Churchill lost the Cabinet of the Prime Minister just ten days after meeting Truman. In the end, it was to turn out that Truman wasn't the only leader in the world who came to the conference handicapped.

The first time they met, Truman and Churchill spoke for over two hours. Churchill left the conference confident about his ability to succeed as the next American President. Truman however did not feel as enthused by the performance of his British counterpart. Though he felt that Churchill was a great leader with a shrewdness that was obvious, Truman felt that the British Premier had tried to impress him overly. His impression of Churchill was, however, likely to never last for the duration of their collaboration.

Joseph Stalin, it would prove, was one day early to The Potsdam Conference due to a minor heart attack. Therefore, Truman chose to travel through Berlin. Berlin in the 16th of July in the afternoon. Truman visited with American soldiers at camp in Berlin within Berlin's American sector. When he returned to his trip, Truman saw the full magnitude of the destruction caused to Berlin the city itself. One of the biggest cities of the world was ruin, and millions of citizens left without their homes and family members. Five thousand civilians were murdered in Allied bombings and tens of hundreds of thousands were raped and attacked by Soviet forces after having eliminated the Nazis. Truman would later write in his diary that Truman was later to write in his journal that Truman "never saw such destruction" prior to his trip to Berlin.

The 16th of July was an even more significant day in American historical records due to what was happening within New Mexico. The next morning, the researchers working on the Manhattan Project exploded their first nuclear bomb. It was an event that was the very first in history when an nuclear weapon had been successful in its construction. Truman and the man who was in charge of the project Secretary of Henry Stimson, Secretary of War Henry Stimson, learned of the announcement later that night but it would take several days for all the details about the explosion to be communicated to Potsdam.

Truman first came into contact with Joseph Stalin the following day at the time that the Soviet president, along with the Foreign Minister Molotov visited his residence. Truman wanted to see Stalin as a good friend however the dictator was to be a foe. The good news however was ahead of any disagreements. Stalin declared to Truman that he was dedicated to delivering on the pledge he made to the president Roosevelt at Yalta in the spring of 1944, which was to make Truman and the Soviet Union declare war on Japan. Stalin said he would declare war at some point in the month of August. Truman and his wife were happy, was informed that Stalin was announcing that Russians planned to take on Manchuria and saw the area as an occupied Chinese territory. This meant that the Soviets were planning to play an active part in the conflict within the Pacific. In the beginning, Truman felt that his relationship with his Soviet counterpart could be pleasant and productive.

Truman wasn't the only person to be enticed by Stalin's charisma. Churchill, Jimmy Byrnes, and Dwight Eisenhower had been impressed. The main reason for an optimistic impression that powerful leaders of the world had upon first having a meeting with Joseph Stalin was that little was made of the crimes that he committed on the home front. In the years and months following did Western officials realize the severity of the brutality of Stalin particularly on the people he was able to control. Stalin's deliberate hunger strike, Katyn Forest Massacre, shocking brutality of Stalin's secret police and the millions in labour camps for a short time were obscured, hidden by Stalin's charismatic personality and all-out military alliance with Western powerhouses. When the war was coming to an end, greater focus would be given to the immorality of Stalin's domestic actions.

In the very first formal gathering to launch the Potsdam Conference on July 17 the three leaders all brought along a variety of their aides as well as Cabinet members. Churchill was accompanied by Clement Attlee with him, his Labor Party opponent in the election and eventually his successor. He also brought Anthony Eden. Truman introduced Secretary Byrnes as well as former United States Ambassador to the Soviet Union Joseph Davies. Stalin also brought Molotov along with his upcoming Foreign Minister Andrey Vyshinsky. Both Churchill as well as Stalin recommended to have Truman be the chairman of the meeting. Though little was accomplished during this first conference, the leadership agreed that they would delegate the majority of the controversial issues on foreign policy to the Foreign Ministers of their respective countries. After the conference Stalin recommended they could divide the German fleet. This was swiftly accepted by Churchill however Truman did not make an official choice. Despite the anxiety of Truman however, the three leaders managed to cooperate and be familiar on the very first day of the meeting, and came to some agreements however, they made minor decisions.

Numerous issues, including Truman's idea of forming the Council of Foreign Ministers representing all the major powerhouses, were assigned to foreign ministers to take care of. In addition, Stalin had confirmed his intent to declare war on Japan.

Truman reported to Churchill on the next day of the success of America in testing an nuclear bomb. After lunching together with Churchill, Truman then proceeded to meet Stalin at the quarters of his residence, and he requested Truman to be a part of having lunch. The three leaders resuming their meetings later that day tensions grew because Stalin determined to make outcomes of the war lasting. There was a first dispute over the German problem. Churchill and Truman tried to establish German territorial boundaries as the ones it was before the war however Stalin believed that they ought to accept Germany in the way it is currently formed, thereby allowing additional territory to be annexed through the Soviets. Even though there was a vigorous discussion, no issue was settled in the initial day of talks.

When the Conference was re-convened in the morning the next day, The President Truman stated to his fellow leaders that the president was not ready to sign a contract for immediately dividing the Germany navy. Truman declared that he supported the idea division into three groups according to what Churchill or Stalin had previously suggested, however only after the victory of Japan. In addition, following a debate between the foreign ministers Truman stated that since his colleagues were skeptical about the possibility of allowing China to become an immediate part of the Council of Foreign Ministers, only the United States, Great Britain, Russia, and France are eligible, and with possible China becoming a member at a later time. The two Churchill and Stalin were in agreement.

The second issue that was on the agenda for next day's conference was as always, Germany. The consensus was that any discussions about Germany should start with a premise that Germany's borders prior to 1937 would be deemed to include the entirety of Germany and any gains in territorial territory that Hitler's Nazis were not considered in the calculation. Any other decisions were delayed to a later time, and leaders started to talk about the direction of Poland. Stalin recommended that all money as well as military assets at the disposal of the government of Poland in exile within London be handed over to the temporary Warsaw administration, which was later discovered to be created under the influence from the Soviet Union, although he refused to acknowledge the reality. The Soviets were clearly looking to acquire the tools and property of more than 150 thousand people that were in the Polish army that represented the exiled government regardless of the fact that the troops were supplied with supplies by British as well as American troops. Churchill quickly began to deliver his own monologue. He reminded his fellow soldiers of the fact that Great Britain had accepted a huge burden by offering a permanent home to Poland's administration during wartime as well as ensuring that all finances of the state were frozen, as if they were part of the assets belonging to the prior war government of Poland. Churchill was also able to offer Polish soldiers who been fighting alongside allies with an opportunity to be granted British citizenship. This was something Churchill was unable to undo. The three leaders subsequently chose to leave the matter up to their ministers for foreign affairs.

The day three of talks started with a talk by Anthony Eden on the progress the foreign ministers have achieved in establishing the areas of agreement. Eden presented the heads with the final version of Truman's original German suggestion that was accepted by all. The Prime Minister Churchill was then able to raise the issue of Spain who's fascist dictatorship was among the few government that survived in the spirit that was Hitler's Germany as well as Mussolini's Italy. Great Britain, Churchill proclaimed that he was dismayed at the brutality that was the Franco regime but resisted the notion of severing relationships with a government which had not done anything to hurt one of the Allied nations. In addition, breaking relations with the Franco regime could establish a potentially dangerous precedent diplomatically that would be harmful to the next generation. Truman was delighted to bring the attention of Franco's atrocities in his country however, relations shouldn't be cut off completely. Truman was in agreement with Churchill and was wary of the likelihood of sparking another civil war within the country that went in turmoil during the past two decades. Stalin asserted that the Franco fascist government was forced upon the Spanish populace by Mussolini as well as Hitler who desired Churchill as well as Truman to agree to discredit the dictatorship, but not end the relationship completely. Churchill and Stalin came to an impasse which led to the matter being delayed for a future date.

Truman was back in Berlin on July 20 and this time he addressed his audience within the American section as the country's flag was raised. It was similar to the flag been flying in Washington during the attack of Pearl Harbor. The flag symbolized, Truman declared, of the American victory against a determined opponent, a victory which he believed could turn out to mark the beginning in the quest for peace in the world. Truman said that the war was the result of fighting for peace one that was something that the Americans continued to pursue aggressively within Japan. In contrast to Russians however, Americans United States did not expect to gain territory after victory in the war however, it was a way to secure prosperity and peace in Europe and around the globe and hoped to stop a catastrophic conflict to come in the near future.

General Eisenhower was invited to join Truman when he visited Berlin The President astonished the Allied commander with his offer his support in the event of a run for the presidency in 1948. Truman held firm, right up until 1952 the year 1952, that Eisenhower was an Democrat. The eventual displeasure with Eisenhower's party choice could later cause a rift between them. In the course of that visit, however, Eisenhower ruled out challenging Truman to the presidency in 1948, and pledging his goal was to make sure that Truman was able to win re-election.

The next day brought news that revealed the full extent the effectiveness in the bomb which was exploded at New Mexico days earlier. Its power and power exceeded what scientists could have imagined. The blast was visible at a distance of nearly two hundred miles from the testing site, and was heard for as far as 100 miles. Truman was delighted with the announcement, since both Truman and Secretary Byrnes were of the opinion that possessing a nuclear weapon could help them when negotiating with Russians greatly. They were also very happy by the fact that $2 billion the federal government had invested in the Manhattan Project had been well used. In addition, due to the test that was successful of the nuclear bomb America could now boast of a weapon with the ability to force surrender from Japan without American forces having to enter Japan. Churchill was the first to learn of the magnitude of the bomb's effectiveness that day later and was equally thrilled.

The leaders retreated to the negotiating table they immediately sank into a rift over matters like the puppet Soviet governments of Romania, Bulgaria, and Finland as well as the issue of the borders between Germany and Poland. Truman was disgusted by the fact that Russia was able to unilaterally alter the boundaries between Germany as well as Poland without consultation with others Great Powers. Truman would have preferred to make use of the borders of Poland in 1937, just like what had happened to Germany however Stalin insists that all the Germans close to the borders had fled to the west. The territory would be transferred to Poland that was in the hands of The Soviet Union. Stalin added that the area in question was a good place to live, and had previously been a source of power for the German economy and was therefore appropriate to give it over to the Poles to keep any Germans from ever recovering significant control over the area. Churchill claimed that this could result in the loss of arable land which the Germans had to protect from massive starvation, and Truman fully agreed. Despite the lively discussion however, the main problems were left to be resolved however Stalin acknowledged that the Soviets could be convinced to permit the press to be present at the coming Polish elections.

On the 22nd of July, while still in Potsdam, Truman was confronted with other choices that needed to be taken regarding the use of nuclear weapons in Japan. Secretary Stimson wanted to see Truman as President select the military's areas of attack, and his initial suggestion was Hiroshima and Hiroshima, which Truman was willing to accept. Following that, Truman decided on drafting the warning declaration, commonly called the Potsdam Declaration, calling on Japan to once more agree for an unconditional surrender it was issued by Allied leadership on July 26. Truman and his advisers reached a consensus to have a nuclear bomb be deployed on Japan on the same day they wrote the declaration. That was July 27. However, the specifics were in the process of being decided. Truman believed that the bomb was going been used to prevent America from suffering hundreds or thousands of victims in an invasion from the ground. Churchill along with Truman's advisors supported the usage of the bomb as did the majority of America's researchers who worked with the bomb.

Truman was officially notified Stalin that he had discovered the nuclear weapon on July 24 however, he was unclear about what exactly it was and about his plans for attacking Japan. On the same day, tensions with the top leaders heated up as Stalin insistently asked both the Americans as well as the British to accept the legitimacy of Russian puppet governments of Eastern Europe. However, Truman insists to insist that the United States could not recognize the legitimacy of the government that were in Romania, Bulgaria, and Hungary since representatives had not yet been granted access to these countries to observe the conditions. America could recognize these government only when they gained access to those countries and Truman insists that they be democratic. This was something Stalin was against regardless of the fact that the two countries had agreed on this at Yalta. A democratically elected government is the only one that will be eligible to be a member of to the United Nations, although Stalin claimed that the other members, for instance Argentina and Brazil, were the same as those Soviet Allied governments of Eastern Europe. Churchill sought an agreement for the admission of Italy to the United Nations However, there was no deal to be found.

While the discussions between President Truman and his advisers regarding the possibility of using the nuclear weapons continued. Truman made a decision that a nuclear weapon would be used against Japan towards the start of August. However, it would also fall over an area where there were at the very least strategic targets for military, not only civilians. Meanwhile, Truman, Churchill, and Stalin came back to the table for negotiations, re-examining the issue of Italy as well as Eastern Europe on July 25. Truman and Churchill both spoke out in favor accepting Italy in the United Nations, as well with other ex- Nazi allies from the Baltics. They both reaffirmed they believed that Romania, Bulgaria and Hungary as well as other countries that were subordinate to Russian control, should not be admitted into the United Nations until they had created democratically elected governments. This was agreed upon at Yalta. Stalin refuted this claim by pointing out that Italy was yet to choose an elected government and therefore Truman's argument about accepting Soviet countries that were occupied into the United Nations after they had established a government that was democratic was a non-issue. Secretary

Byrnes However, she clarified his American and British policy by reminding Stalin that Italy has open borders in contrast, Soviet states that were under occupation were not able to allow Western Allies into their country.

One of the major issues that persisted throughout the whole conference was that Truman and Stalin were in disagreement about the definition of a democratic government. Truman maintained that a democratically elected government was one elected by people through open fair and free elections. Stalin declared that every political system that was not one of the fascists was democratic. He argued that the Soviet Union and its satellite nations all had democratically elected administrations. A disagreement of this kind was not resolved between the two major nations until after it was Cold War ended more than forty years later.

Truman was then able to present his plan for internationalization of waterways throughout the globe, and will grant every nation access to all major waterways. Churchill was seen to have a positive view of Truman's plan, however Stalin did not want to sign a contract for such an arrangement.

Winston Churchill left the Conference in the night of July 25, and returned to London to discover the outcomes from the British general elections that took place earlier in that month. Churchill was confident of winning easily and he promised his fellow leaders they would be back at the Conference within a couple of days. When the world's other leaders were informed of Churchill's shocking defeat, Stalin again put the Conference in a standstill, hesitant to confront an opponent who was a different one with the name of Clement Attlee. After the demise of Roosevelt and Churchill as leaders of the trio of Great Power wartime alliance, only Stalin was left as the only relic from the generation rapidly being replaced within politically-oriented circles. When Attlee returned to the summit on July 28 to succeed Churchill during the talks between Allied heads, Truman was far from pleased with Churchill's successor. Ernest Bevin had also been named as the successor to Anthony Eden as the British Foreign Secretary.

Truman chose to issue his Potsdam Declaration on July 26 the day following the delivery of a nuclear bomb that was handed over to American troops in the Pacific in anticipation of its use. Furthermore It was of primary significance to note that Truman, Atlee, and Chiang Kai-shek, the Chairman of the Chinese government, have signed the document which suggested that the Japanese are doomed to fail as all of the Great Powers, along with the Chinese all united in seeking Japan's unconditional submission to Allied forces. After an eventual Japanese surrender in the aftermath of the surrender, it was announced that the Great Powers announced that they were calling on Japan to grant free speech rights, restore the policy of tolerance for religion and to elect a peaceful government. After that, the invading troops would leave the nation. Documents were thrown by American planes over Japan informing all the people of Japan in the event that Japanese militaries that controlled the state were not likely to notify the citizens of the threat that was posed from Allied forces. The Japanese Prime Minister was able to dismiss the threats posed by Allies. It was nevertheless an important one.

President Truman became aware of the vote which was held within the United States Senate on the acceptance of the United Nations treaty on July 28. The vote in favor of this United Nations charter was overwhelming in the Senate, with 89 Senators supporting being a part of the group, and only two opposing. This was a huge success for Truman as President. Truman because he had achieved what had been out of President Wilson for decades. Truman was overjoyed with the fact that the United Nations organization which he and Roosevelt have fought for could finally be an actual reality. In a short statement sent in the press, Truman proclaimed that "it is extremely satisfying that the Senate approved the United Nations Charter by a almost unanimous decision. The decision of the Senate significantly advances the cause for world peace."

Truman's final authorization for the deployment of a nuclear weapon to Japan as well as the weapon's specifically targeted target, was granted on July 31.

The Potsdam Conference was expected to close on August 2 however, when the talks ended over the course of the last days of July Truman ended up with only a handful of achievements. Apart from securing Stalin's commitment to declare war against Japan Truman had not been able to settle the German as well as Polish issues as well as had not yet had a commitment renewed by the Soviets to organize open and democratic elections throughout Eastern Europe. In spite of this lack of advancement however, there was a broad agreement that Truman did a fantastic job when dealing with the and the other Allied leaders, even though relationships between United States and Russia appeared to be about to decline.

According to what Stalin was quoted by Truman at the beginning of his tenure that it was going to be tougher for the two countries to maintain their alliance in time of peace. However, they were able to reach an agreement that the German state would be removed from military service, and during the transition it will continue to remain under the protection of Allied forces.

Truman and Stalin were in agreement to have the Nuremburg war crimes trials in Germany in the first place, and also arranged specific reparations for members of the Soviet Union because of the sacrifices made by the country during the fight against Nazis in the course of war or at least in the last four years. The Russians were to continue their terrifying presence within Eastern Europe, as the realities of the situation the ground was that Western nations had no option in settling the scenario. Three leaders were able to reach an agreement on the proportion of German reparations would be paid to the Soviets will receive and at the end of the day, they agreed on Poland's western border.

Truman began to hate Stalin at the close at the end of this conference. Truman considered Stalin's Soviet Union as a police state and had even informed his mom that he thought Stalin was cruel. Yet he was unable to avoid the charm of Stalin, and believed that he was an individual that would be faithful to his word. In reality, Truman was to discover later that this kind of thinking was extremely naive on its side, despite the fact that a number of other were fooled by Stalin's warm and friendly manner. After he left the office did Truman be able to speak about the numerous wrongs he had committed during the conference. The most notable was among being his innate trust of Stalin. Soviet leader to stick to his commitment to his.

Truman was able to leave Potsdam to go to Washington on the 2nd of August. In his return journey Truman ate dinner with the King George VI en route to the Augusta close to Plymouth. The Augusta was intended to ferry Truman back to his home over into the Atlantic Ocean. After arriving in the ocean, Truman informed the press about the existence of an nuclear weapon. One of his major concerns was the possibility that other countries would shortly acquire nuclear weapons however, most believed that they would not. Soviet Union would take possibly longer than a decade create one of their own. Then, they'd explode their first nuclear weapon in 1949, which was well into the start of Cold War.

Hiroshima was hit on the night of the 6th of August 1945 even though the date was the 5th of August in Washington. Following the first time that there was an nuclear weapon ever in human history, Truman was informed of the developments while eating lunch with a few colleagues as well as personnel of the team. Secretary Stimson told Truman as well as Secretary of State Byrnes that the nuclear weapon was far more effective than the people that were used by the military. Truman exuberantly awaited the news, believing that this was the last shock for that the Japanese will need to accept an unconditional surrender. It would also save the lives of the hundreds of thousands in American people who were likely to be a victim of a ground invasion into Japan themselves. Truman as well as his advisors in no way aware about the severity of physical harm done to their foes, however they issued a threat to hit the Japanese with additional nuclear weapons should the Japanese government refuse to surrender. The majority of them believed that the Japanese will quickly reconsider their policies in light of a threatening danger to their military. It is estimated that more than eighty-thousand residents from Hiroshima died upon the explosion, while some tens of thousands further damaged by the resulting radiation.

Some were not thrilled. Some worried that the deployment of a nuclear weapon could lead the world to the new era of hazardous war. The thought that cities could be destroyed in a matter of minutes with a single bomb was terrifying at best.

In a broadcast of a speech from the cruise ship via the radio for the American citizens on the exact day as the nuclear bomb fell upon Hiroshima, Truman attempted to justify his decision to use this dangerous weapon. Truman told Americans who were listening to him across the nation that the bomb was employed "to shorten the agony of war, in order to save the lives of thousands and thousands of young Americans." Truman declared that the United States, Truman proclaimed will continue dropping nuclear bombs upon Japan until they surrendered completely.

Truman came back to Truman's White House on August 8. Truman was absent for more than a month and was delighted to be back to his home in the United States. The second time a nuclear bomb was unleashed against Japan in Nagasaki. Nagasaki, Truman was in the White House to follow the events more carefully. Nagasaki was a death zone. Nagasaki was almost as large as those who died in Hiroshima. Truman was grieving privately over the death of a large number of civilians, realized that his actions were needed in order to pressure the radical Japanese military and government to surrender. Truman finally urged Japanese civilians to at leaving major sites of industry in order to safeguard their own. The Japanese government was issued an extremely serious warning on the evening of August 5 but were not willing to surrender. A second nuclear weapon in the midst of Japan could prove more psychologically damaging.

The same day Truman was to return home Washington on August 8th it was reported by the Russians that they had plans to declare war against Japan on the next day. This message was relayed through Ambassador Averell Harriman. The ambassador was in contact with Vyacheslav Molotov, the Soviet Foreign Minister Vyacheslav Molotov. The latter came in to notify the American Ambassador about Stalin's decision.

Truman decided to inform the American populace about the Soviet government's stance through a press release at inside the White House.

There was news of a deal offer made by the Japanese management on the 10th of August. It was made through the states that were neutral, Switzerland as well as Sweden. The issue of contention was thought to revolve around the role that of the Emperor Hirohito was to assume following the outbreak of war. The Japanese tried to prevent the Emperor on his feet which seemed to be the sole issue standing from an unconditional Japanese surrender. When Truman, Churchill, and Stalin were all in agreement that unconditional surrender was the main goal, Truman began to ponder whether or not he should allow the Emperor to remain at his place. While tens of thousands of Russian soldiers invaded

Manchuria Secretary Stimson believed in reaching an agreement with Hirohito who was left to his own devices however, others, such as Secretary Byrnes did not want to compromise on the issue of disagreement. A lot of Americans were still adamant about seeing the Emperor Hirohito as the central figure of the military-oriented Japanese government they had pledged to defeat. However, ultimately it was for the President to choose a plan of actions.

Truman determined that the Emperor was kept in his place however his position within the nation was tightly regulated through Truman and the United States. Truman was effectively transformed into the leader of the state by name. Truman's plan won the backing from the British, Australians, Chinese as well as Soviets. The situation appeared to suggest that Truman's plan was that the United States would not be threatened with the deployment of a second nuclear bomb and Truman believed that a swift surrender would result in less Soviet troops advancing in the region. Their history of destruction throughout Europe and expanding their global policies were then widely known. General Douglas MacArthur was chosen to be the supreme General of the Allied Command for The Allied Powers in Asia, and was given the task of managing the prevailing situation in Japan. In China the public were already being expressed about what the imminent withdrawal of Japanese forces would mean to the possibility of establishing and stabilizing a administration. It was the consensus of the international community Chiang Kai-shek's army must take over China. However, Communist rebels warned of launching into civil conflict. In the meantime, Soviet Union already appeared to be ready to support Chiang

Kai-shek's Communist forces of China instead of seeking the moderate and stable administration that the allies previously endorsed.

The Japanese announced unconditional surrender to Allied forces on the 14th of August in the United States, and Truman immediately informed the media about the fact that the war was finished. Then, he broadcast a message to the American citizens to announce that war was officially been declared over. Truman as well as his wife Bess went out of his White House to wave to fans on the front lawn and celebrate the victory along with peers. Harry Truman, the everyday American who grew up on the farm of the middle of Missouri and ended up in the White House, had won the battle. In a speech to his the people who supported him, Truman hailed the moment as an important day in the history of liberty across the world and the moment when "fascism and police government ceases in the world."

At the point that the war was officially declared over on August 14th, Truman had been in his office only three months and 2 days. In the time Truman had had meetings together with the two most influential people on earth to discuss the future of Europe and was the president of the United Nations, oversaw the success of the Manhattan Project, and issued the command to use nuclear weapons on two Japanese cities. It was the first and to date only occasion in the history of mankind where such a weapon has been utilized. Harry Truman was the man who made what may be the most difficult decision of all time in letting the magnitude of destruction that occurred through only one nuclear weapon. But Truman was the first person to claim that he was just a normal American that was placed in a unique situation. He was up to the challenge and steered the rise to America United States into the role as the most powerful country around the globe.

The conflict with the Soviets but, it was to persist. Truman and Stalin dispute over the fate of the Kurile Islands, then a part of Japan prior to the time that war was officially over. Truman accepted the Soviets being in control of the islands, but he demanded in return that they have the right to maintain the American base on the island to serve commercial and war-time purposes. Stalin was eventually able to allow Truman and the United States maintain a temporary base in the region however these types of disagreements would soon become commonplace in the future.

Chapter 8: A Year of Discontent

In the year that Truman's presidency ended, and the Second World War came to an end, Truman was able to concentrate on domestic policies for the first time during his presidency. Truman was, in several ways an essentially New Deal Democrat. Truman wanted to increase the standard of living, as well as unemployment insurance as well as crop insurance and many others liberal legislative ideas. However, Truman was soon to realize that the politicians at Capitol Hill were much more accommodating and supportive during the midst of war, and his initial opposition to the Congress is about to be revealed. Truman's plans appeared far larger than Roosevelt's and he quickly sparked the ire of the majority of traditional Democrats.

Truman was determined to prevent chaos which had erupted following The First

World War. Twelve million American soldiers returned from battle in 1945. The majority of them were required to seek work. American's economy was booming prior to the war but some were concerned that the growth would never be sustained after the end of production during wartime. With all the troops fighting in the war, unemployment dropped to an all-time low of 2 percent by the close of war. However, the addition of twelve million additional employees would certainly cause the unemployment rate to increase. Some, including some members of Truman's Cabinet were of the opinion that Americans will be forced back to confront the same issues that had were affecting the nation prior to the war started in 1939.

The majority of those who were worried had a point: workers went in a nationwide strike in search of higher wages. the majority of soldiers returned and discovered a housing crisis. Congress hesitated to take action but, though the subject of the economy was not Truman's forte however, he determined to act to express his love for the American citizens.

A number of changes to the personnel in the government took place in the time after the conclusion of the war. The most notable change was being the departure of Henry Stimson as Secretary of War. Stimson was then close to 85 and ready to take his retirement after decades in public service. Truman presented him with the Distinguished Service Medal. The same honor was awarded for General George Marshall, who had served as the Army's Chief of Staff during the conflict. The General was also retiring but Truman was later to ask for him to resume public service, as an advisor to China Secretary of State and eventually, Secretary of Defense.

Chaos and disorganization was beginning to afflict in the White House as Truman's inexperience was beginning to surface. Truman had many issues to address and was striving to do everything simultaneously, always frustrated at the inability of Congress to move. Further problems were brewing in the field of labor. In the wake of declaring his acceptance of moderate wage increases, Truman was convinced by lawmakers in Congress to take a more stern stance against unions. But his firm stance only held off strikes until the end of about a month. This was a huge disappointment for all those affected.

When an American Embassy to China abruptly quit due to his argument that he was a supporter within China's State Department for the Chinese Communist rebels Truman requested George Marshall to end his six-day vacation and go to China as soon as possible.

The Council of Foreign Ministers, that was established during the Potsdam Conference to include the United States, Great Britain as well as the Soviet Union, met for the first time in September 1945. Three nations initially determined to include France as well as China could participate in the meeting, however they could only participate in things that directly affected their own interests. The foreign minister of the Soviet Union, Molotov, was now threating to renege to his words and stop the conference in case France and China weren't removed from any conversations that were not related to their national interests completely and instead allowed to take part but not voting. Secretary Byrnes made a call to Truman at the time of his visit to London just eleven days after the conference been inaugurated, and was required to pleading with President Truman to reach out to Joseph Stalin directly to prevent the Soviets from leaving the gathering completely. Following the meeting, Stalin was unable to change Molotov's stance, the meeting was abruptly brought to an close on October 2 leading many observers to an impression that the conference was an overall fail. Additional problems for the council were revealed when even though there was a consensus among the main powers to ensure in which all foreign troops were to be removed from Iran in early 1946 Russia continued to send additional troops to the country instead of removing them. Stalin's Soviets were very unwilling to ever fulfill their commitments.